M000033748

365

Positive Strategies
for Single Parenting

"The focus is on the burdens of single parenting. But it also superbly expresses the basics of the 3R's of all successful journeys to adulthood–responsibility, respect, and restraint. Bottom line? *365 Positive Strategies for Single Parenting* is must reading for anyone interfacing with children."

—Don Martin
TV Talk Show Host, WHHI-TV
Hilton Head Island, South Carolina

"This book is a survival kit for single parents. The stories and strategies provide valuable insight into raising children with an absent parent."

—Phillip J. McLaughlin
Associate Professor of Special Education
University of Georgia

"This book is from the laboratory of life. No one can dispute it because Monica and Susan have lived it."

—Austin Parker
MSSW, ACSW

"In a time when there are many single parents, families will find *365 Positive Strategies for Single Parenting* to be a useful and supportive guide. Brown and Simmons address in a refreshingly positive manner the many responsibilities and pressures that single parents face."

—Bobby E. Parham
Georgia Congressman

"*365 Positive Strategies* offers to single parents the humor, logic, wit, and pragmatism that will help any solo parent be successful . . . and sane!"

—Judy Thigpen
Principal, Cobb County School District, Georgia

"Monica and Susan have the expertise in education and child development, but more importantly, they have lived the life of the single parent–which is a vital ingredient of this book."

—Jerome Mersberger, M.D.
Board Certified Family Practice
Board Certified Emergency Room Medicine

Positive Strategies
for Single Parenting

Susan B. Brown, Ph.D.
Monica Simmons, M.Ed.

PEAKE ROAD
Macon, Georgia

ISBN 1-57312-177-0

365 Positive Strategies for Single Parenting

Susan B. Brown
Monica Simmons

Copyright © 1998
Peake Road

Smyth & Helwys Publishing, Inc.
6316 Peake Road
Macon, Georgia 31210-3960
1-800-747-3016

All rights reserved.
Printed in the United States of America.

The paper used in this publication meets the minimum
requirements of American National Standard for Information
Sciences—Permanence for Printed Library Materials,
ANSI Z39.48–1984.

Library of Congress Cataloging-in-Publication Data

Brown, Susan.
  365 positive strategies for single parenting/
  Susan B. Brown, Monica Simmons.
  p.   cm.
  Includes bibliographical references.
  ISBN 1-57312-177-0 (alk. paper)
  1. Single parents.
  2. Child rearing.
  3. Parenting.
  4. Parenting, Part-time.
  5. Child development.
  I. Simmons, Monica. II. Title.
  HQ759.915.B76 1998
  649'.1'0243—dc21

                                                97-50024
                                                CIP

To my parents for their support
To Matt and Dan
for sharing their mom with the computer
—S. B. B.

To my mother and father who are both single parents
To Manley and Rachael who make my home festive
—M. S. S.

Special thanks to Austin Parker, A.C.S.W.,
for his mentorship.

Contents

Preface

When you enter the world of single parenting, you embark on a solo journey. The journey will have reminders along the way that you are alone. There are more hats to wear than you can manage. In many cases you will have to be the resident mother, resident father, tax accountant, taxi driver, school and church liaison, and chief cook and bottle washer. You become a jack-of-all-trades, attempting to master it all. You must earn the dinner, cook the dinner, clean the house, pay the bills, budget the household, plan the entertainment, keep the schedule of events, and hold down at least one job and sometimes two. In addition, you face the difficult adjustment of being alone. The desire for someone to lean on or share with can be overwhelming.

If raising children is considered a labor of love, then raising children alone should be considered an act of the greatest magnitude. The positive trade-off of single parenting is the focus of this book. It evolved as we shared our trials and tribulations as single parents and researched the extent of the single-parent experience and the unmet needs of this population. In it we share positive strategies you can use to make single parenting the most happy and rewarding experience for you and your children. You will miss the joys of sharing your children's growth on a daily basis with another parent, but you will develop a sense of accomplishment no other task can give you. Remember, it is not reality as perceived by others that colors our lives, but our own perception of that reality.

This book will help you perceive single parenting as a task that not only can be done alone, but can be done very well alone. This doesn't mean it is easy. This is not a task for the weak-hearted. But step by step, bit by bit, you can piece together your most important values and weave the most beautiful single-parent family. You and your children can become, thread by thread, a unique fabric with the strength to withstand the hard times and the love to rejoice in the good times.

To aid in your task as a single parent, we begin each chapter with a story pertaining to a particular age group or parenting issue, followed by introductory comments on the topic and then discussion of general parenting strategies. Each strategy contains specific questions and answers to help you maintain a balance between meeting your needs and those of your children, thus making you a more efficient parent. Learning the reasons behind the strategies will prepare you for the unexpected. This book will provide you with both—strategies and knowledge.

For the purposes of this book, we have chosen to call the parent who is not present in the home on a daily basis the "absent parent." We could have used the terms "noncustodial parent," the "missing parent," the "nonresident parent," or the "other parent." Absent parent means no more than that: the parent who is physically absent in the custodial home. We do not use the term "ex-spouse" or "spouse" because it excludes a large portion of the single-parent population who are single mothers by choice, whether by adoption or never marrying the absent parent. We use the term "parent" rather than "mother" or "father" in every instance possible that could apply to either the mother or the father, although the overwhelming majority of single parents in the United States today are single mothers. And to send a more personal message, in most cases, we use singular terms to refer to children, and alternate usage of male and female pronouns.

We must caution you of numerous reports in the media that highlight the problems of children from single-parent families, but it is worthy to note that some studies on children show single-parent children to be more dependable in the work force, more responsible, and more competent than their two-parent peers. Other studies show no differences in school success between children from single-parent or two-parent families. Thus, children from single-parent homes can achieve positive outcomes equal to children from dual-parent homes. Your job is to guide your child toward positive outcomes.

But remember, there is no perfect parent. Eliminate energy wasters, such as guilt, from your parenting. Instead, look forward. The 21st century will change the parenting styles for the future, and single parenting, as a majority parenting style, is just as individual as each parent and each child. The positive outcomes for children in this generation from single-parent families will gloriously change the status quo forever! With all of your priorities in order, a sense of confidence about your single parenting skills, lots of positive strategies, and the expectation of positive results, you will have the reward of happy, healthy, successful children.

Developmental Differences

Jack was oblivious to the panic in his mother's voice as she asked for cooperation in dressing for preschool. He was totally absorbed, playing on the floor in his room with trucks, cars, and action figures. His clothes were laid out on the bed, along with his shoes, but he was in a world full of army men and aliens. Besides, he didn't want to go to school.

Stephanie, on the other hand, was in her bedroom, almost dressed. She had carefully chosen purple stockings and a red velvet dress. Pink summer "jellies" graced her feet. The ribbon she put sideways in her long brown hair was full of shiny silver dots on white satin. She also had remembered a headband made of pink cloth with tiny pearls sewn on it. Lots of shiny plastic bangle bracelets clanked as she busily packed teddy bears and dolls in a pink patent leather Beauty and the Beast™ backpack while listening intently to her mother's directions. She was in tune with her mother's mood and aware that she had to hurry.

To the young mother's dismay, she came upon Jack still playing. With only minutes to get out the door, she panicked. Thinking she would have to dress Stephanie as well, she grabbed Jack and pulled him out of his pajama shirt and pants at the same time. She suddenly felt overwhelmed with the enormity of raising two children alone. Just as a lump of frustration began to settle into her throat, Stephanie walked in with her raincoat and backpack on, announcing she was ready for school. The mother looked over to see that not only was Stephanie ready for school, but she was ready for anything!

The mother looked at both children and began to laugh at herself and with her children. Jack was 4; Stephanie was 2. Stephanie was not only competing with her brother, but was outperforming every time! Later, however, Stephanie would work for her grades in school while Jack, with a memory like a steel trap, would "breeze through" school.

Children do not and should not develop in exactly the same way or at the same rate. Norms, or what is considered normal, are merely guides to the way behavior develops in general. These guides to behavior are better considered as a sequence rather than a timetable. Within this pattern of development is a vast area of individual differences called developmental differences. There are universal guidelines for growth and development. The details, however, are determined by parent-child interactions, the environment provided for children at each stage of their development, and children's own developmental "clocks."

From the moment of birth, children display vast individual differences that determine parental reactions to them. They are born with certain hereditary characteristics, such as hair color, eye color, height, and body build. They inherit these characteristics from their parents. Heredity plays an important part in children's development. Some children are precocious like their parents, whereas some children are late bloomers.

Children can be better understood by realizing that this blueprint of genetics determines their characteristics. As one farmer simply put it, "You don't order them from Sears and Roebuck." True. You may have wanted a girl but got a boy. You may have wanted an athlete but got a musician. Those things are beyond your control as a parent, but you do have control over how you choose to deal with them. This control is called the environment.

The environment children live in is the home you make for them. The immediate family and the home are primary shapers of the personality of children. Children are also shaped by the environment of the larger family. Extended family members have a great impact on children and the development of their attitudes and values. The neighborhood, country, and world also influence their lives. In addition, court cases and politics of the time can give them attitudes and qualities that are unique to their generation.

Understand the importance of developmental differences.

You may not be a perfect parent. Everyone makes mistakes. You do the best you can through the stages of childhood. The most important job in the world, that of parenting, comes with no instructions. How do you know what to do? How do you do the right things? Parenting is a hard enough job with two parents at the helm. When you are a single parent, the job can be overwhelming. How can you raise happy, healthy children alone?

One way to enhance your parenting skills is to learn about the differences in children's thinking at various ages and stages by reading about developmental differences. At each stage your child must master a new developmental task, such as standing, before moving on to a new challenge, such as walking. Consulting books on child development will help you know if you are doing the right things and if your child is on the right track. You can find out if your child's behavior is normal by simply reading what the experts say. This knowledge will relieve stress for you and your child and will also help you face new developmental tasks as a single-parent family.

(1) What can I generally expect in my child's development?

Physical development proceeds from head to toes. Neck muscles develop first, and then the trunk and legs. First a baby supports his own head, then learns to sit, and finally stands. Development also follows a center-to-fingertips direction. First, arms are used in gross motor movement. Later, fine motor control will develop with wrists, fingers, and thumbs. In other words, big movements come first, and small movements come last.

(2) How will my child's thinking vary at different ages?

Jean Piaget, a French psychologist, outlined a model for the development of thinking. In the United States, educators and child psychologists accept Piaget's stages of the development of thinking as the foundation for understanding children. Following is an overview of the stages and ages of development outlined by Piaget.[1]

- *Sensorimotor, 0–2*: Children utilize senses and reflexes to begin understanding the world around them. They use eyes to see, hands to grasp, and mouths to suck. They see themselves as the center of the universe. Objects that cannot be seen no longer exist. The world consists of the here and now.

- *Preoperational, 2–7*: Children prepare for school. They learn to symbolize, or put words together with objects or ideas. Language acquisition develops rapidly. They believe everything has a reason or a purpose, which accounts for thousands of questions. They think the world operates around them and are unable to put themselves in another's place. Therefore, sharing is a typical problem.

- *Concrete operations, 7–12*: Children can manipulate objects and learn to classify objects, events, and time. They are less egocentric and understand that other people's feelings may be different from their own.

- *Formal operations, 11–15*: Children are able to understand increasingly complex and hypothetical problems. They can think with symbols and have the ability to reason scientifically and logically.

(3) How can I help extended family members understand developmental differences in my child?

Ask family members who will spend the most time with your child to attend a single parenting seminar with you. Give them a copy of a child development chart. Discuss your readings with them on a regular basis. Model developmentally appropriate expectations and activities. Decline family invitations to late events when your child would be too tired. Bring toys to occupy her on visits to adult environments.

(4) Should I change my expectations of my child as he grows older?

The stages of childhood are: newborn, infancy, toddler, preschool, school age, and adolescence. Each stage has specific characteristics but also merges with the previous and following stages. All children follow a general pattern of human growth and development, but in their own unique way. Your expectations for your child will change as he passes from one developmental stage to the next. You can't take your toddler for a 4-hour shopping expedition during the Christmas rush and expect good behavior. Your teenager, however, would enjoy this experience, but would prefer to share it with friends.

Understand differences in response to family change.

Children react in different ways to changes in the family. When a parent leaves the home, your child will perceive it as a loss. He will mourn the loss of the family as it was. His reactions to this loss will be affected by his age and developmental stage.

(5) Does the age of my child affect her response to accepting the loss of a parent?

A young infant may not be as affected by the loss of a parent as a toddler who is establishing gender-role identification and developing a strong relationship with both parents. An older child will respond according to her developmental needs. A school-aged child may feel guilt that she caused the parent to leave. An adolescent may feel angry at her parents for their "embarrassing" behavior.

(6) How will my young child understand a loss?

The masters of child development, Piaget and Vygotsky[2], outline the different stages in the development of children's thinking. A young child has a different type of thinking than an older child or an adult. His mind is not a "little adult" mind but is unique at stages along the pathway of development of certain abilities and qualities.

He has not mastered the concepts of time and permanency. He cannot differentiate between fantasy and reality. He may attempt to "wish it away."

(7) Does my child's gender affect his response to the loss of a parent?

Loss of the same-gender parent will be more difficult for your child since he has a need to identify a sex role with that parent. Loss of the opposite-sex parent will impact the development of the ability of your child to maintain positive relationships with members of the opposite sex.

(8) Will stress affect the development of my child?

Changes in family structure, such as the loss of a parent, cause stress. Stress may hinder the development of your child and can create learning blocks for him at school. Stress can also cause physical problems and illness. Your child needs consistency and security, which can be provided by routines that alleviate some stress.

(9) How can I help my child learn stress management?

Model stress management to your child. Learning to manage stress can prepare her for later success. If she sucks her thumb for comfort, teach her more socially acceptable methods of self-comfort. Help her manage stress by focusing on positives, talking to you or a family member who understands, and getting physical exercise.

(10) How will my child behave in response to the "single" part of family change?

Be alert because your child may regress under stress. Her behavior may become immature. She may forget developmental skills she has mastered. A preschooler may return to baby talk. An elementary school child may return to bed-wetting. Notice changes in observable behavior. They are symptoms of feelings your child cannot put into words. Don't punish her for immature behaviors when she is trying to deal with strong emotions. Rather, offer loving acceptance and guide her towards more appropriate behavior.

Encourage
age-appropriate behavior.

Your child wants to please you. Understanding age-appropriate behaviors can help you determine what to expect from him. If you expect too much, he will be frustrated because he does not have the skills to live up to your expectations. If you expect too little, you are not encouraging him to grow and mature.

A child who has strong self-esteem feels he is lovable just the way he is. Providing him with a positive self-image gives him confidence to try new things and the competence to be self-assured. A child who is treated in an authoritarian manner or in a permissive manner will have lower self-esteem than one from a family with rules and guidelines.[3]

It is important to separate love for your child from approval of his behavior. Tell him you love him but that some behaviors are unacceptable. Ignoring the immature behaviors will not eliminate them. Praise your child for mature behaviors. Say, "I like it when you talk like a big boy." Offer him opportunities to show he can handle responsibility. Give verbal and nonverbal demonstration of your love.

(11) What does it mean when my child acts younger than his age?

Your child may regress when things become scary or something bad happens, such as when he suffers a physical or emotional trauma or loss. He may revert to younger behaviors as a means of seeking security.

(12) How should I deal with my child's immature behaviors?

Ignoring immature behaviors will not eliminate them. Teach your child more mature behaviors. Specifically identify the behaviors you prefer. If you notice her making a mannerly introduction and shaking hands with the person she is meeting, at the first opportunity, make a reinforcing statement such as: "You made a good impression on the karate instructor! He sees you as well-mannered and confident."

(13) How can I help my child develop age-appropriate behaviors?

In order to get appropriate behaviors from your child, tell him what he is supposed to *do* rather than how he is expected to *be*. If you want him to act a certain way, be specific. For instance, you are going to the library. You say to your child, "Please be quiet." While in the library he does not speak, or else he speaks only in a whisper. He runs around the stacks of books and up and down the stairs and into the elevator and out, and plays hide-and-seek silently—but he's quiet. He is, amidst the hoopla, following the rule—"*Be* Quiet."

Rather than telling your child to *be* a certain way, tell him what to *do*. Say: "This is the library. People are reading or studying. I am bringing you to the library because you are able to follow the rules. The rules are: do not talk, do not run, do not play, do not make noise. Some things you *can do* are: go to the children's section, look at the books, walk slowly and quietly, respect the other people in the library. I trust you to follow these rules."

These instructions save you the time and embarrassment of chasing down a child in the library. They can also boost your child's confidence. By being specific about expected behavior, you give your child the opportunity to be successful and to receive praise for proper behavior.

(14) How can I get my child to act appropriately?

Your child is influenced most by her home and family. She lives up to the messages that come from the home. These messages reflect a supportive parent—"I am lucky to have you for my child"—or a critical parent—"You are worthless." Your child lives up to what she hears. For example, if you wish to encourage independence, say, "You are a very good helper." You will encourage dependence if you say, "Let me do that for you; it is too hard for you." Provide supportive messages that encourage independence.

(15) When should I reward my child's good behavior?

Reward good behavior as soon as possible. Your child's sense of time is much different from yours. Use coupons for rewards that are to take place in the future. Try not to ask him to postpone getting rewards for too long. He cannot delay gratification for good behavior as long as you can; this is a learned behavior.

(16) What are good reinforcers for my child's behavior?

Praise and attention are the most powerful reinforcers of good behavior. They are also cheap and easy to dispense immediately. Include a few favorite family activities. These can be saved for weekends. Special treats such as time with Mom or Dad to share an activity or inexpensive gifts are also helpful.

(17) Should I use food as a reward for my child's good behavior?

Avoid using food as a reward for good behavior. Giving food rewards can lead to eating problems for your child as she grows older. Overweight children and adults often view food as "comfort." They use it to satisfy needs other than hunger.

(18) How can I prevent behavior problems resulting from sibling rivalry?

You cannot prevent rivalry among children. It is normal behavior. You can minimize it by not comparing siblings to each other in an attempt to get them to perform or conform. Do not say, "Jack ate his dinner, so he's going to grow bigger than you." Statements concerning mealtime, homework, or grades at school create jealousy among siblings and make them compete with each other for your approval. Compare your children only to themselves. Focus on developing your family as a unit. Encourage respect for and support of each other.

Focus on the positive.

An old Chinese proverb states, "I hear and I forget, I see and I remember, I do and I understand." Remember, actions speak louder than words. Giving your child the opportunity to observe you modeling appropriate behaviors is more powerful than any lecture you might give her about values. If you expect appropriate behavior and communicate your belief that your child can meet these expectations, she will become more independent and self-assured.

Your child will thrive when she feels loved and valued. Encouragement and praise provide the building blocks for her self-esteem. Practice giving positive messages daily so it will become automatic. Put a list of positive reminders on the refrigerator or bathroom. If you are not in this habit, start with general positive remarks such as: "You have a really great smile"; "It makes me feel happy when I see you so giggly"; or "You are great kids."

(19) What effects can my positive attitude have on my child?

If you are positive and look for the good in yourself and your child, not only will your child make positive statements, but he will also learn to imitate your attitude and act in positive ways. For instance, research on the positive effects of working mothers on their children show that working mothers model competence to their children. Daughters of working mothers are more self-confident, make better grades, and are more likely to choose careers. Sons and daughters of working mothers are more independent and reliable.[4]

(20) How can I help my child focus on the positive?

Your child will focus on the positive if *you* focus on the positive. Regardless of what you say to do, she will learn to do as you do. If you make loving comments, she will imitate you. She will say, "You are the best mom in the world," or "I love you, Daddy." If you are in the habit of using positive statements, you will be able to see the positive side more quickly during difficult times, and your child will be there to encourage you with positive statements.

(21) What can I do to focus on the positive each day?

Focus on your positive qualities. Take pride in your appearance and skills. Share your time only with positive people. Treat yourself well. Go to the river or a nearby lake and fish from the shore, or just skip stones. Place positive statements throughout your house (mirrors are good places). Collect funny photos of your child from birth to present. Place them in a small album. Look at the book with your child and share a laugh, or pull it out when you're feeling down.

Teach your child to compliment others, especially you and his siblings. Teach him to give praise. You will begin to thrive on his remarks, and he will learn to be gracious. Remark on the good things you see in him, and he will flourish. The happier your child is, the more he will smile—and the more you will smile. The more you smile, the happier and more positive you feel. Each happy thing you do will beget happy things. Soon you will be in the habit of being positive, and you will really feel that way.

Be consistent.

Your single-parent family is often more of a democracy because of the close relationship developed between the you and your child. It's a neat little package, very tight and compact. Your child takes on more responsibility and, therefore, takes a stronger voice in decisions. House rules and family meetings can work very well in this more democratic (not totally democratic) structure.

If your family has been single parent from early on, it has a chance to stabilize by the time your child reaches school age. When a parent leaves a home that has already developed a structure, however, changes in the family structure can crumble your child's sense of security. As a result, your child will test the limits by challenging rules and authority.

Even under the best circumstances, it is hard to be consistent. Therefore, when you are calm and relaxed, establish a plan of action for dealing with inappropriate behavior. Once a behavior problem starts, you may be too stressed to deal with it appropriately. Some degree of democracy is good, but always retain your position of authority. You may become too severe in discipline as you strive to gain control of your life and prove you can handle your child. On the other hand, if guilt dominates, you may become too permissive, trying to make up for the absence of a parent in her life. Too close of a bond can put your child in unnatural roles, those of friend and confidant. This can interfere with her developing independence.

(22) How do I develop a plan of action for becoming consistent with my child?

Write down a set of rules and consequences. Refer to them often, such as in a weekly family meeting. Give your child a chance to talk about issues important to him. Written rules encourage planning, and family meetings encourage consistency.

(23) What does it mean to be consistent with my child?

Being consistent means planning ahead. It means having proactive strategies that anticipate problems. It means following a set of rules and guidelines and enforcing consequences for rule-breaking behavior. It does *not* mean that you will never make exceptions or that you will function as a robot on a rigid and uncompromising schedule. It means that you will post rules, have meetings about rule enforcement, and administer agreed-upon consequences to rule-breaking behavior.

(24) How can I be consistent when my child has two homes?

"Grandma always yells at us about the dogs," said Bo.

"I know, but she always bakes chocolate cake and strawberry shortcake. I love it when she makes spaghetti," Leigh added.

"Yeah," said her brother, "The funniest part is when she yells about the dogs, but I think she's the best cook."

"She likes to watch us from the window when we play outside. And remember, I love her bird feeder; there's always birds there."

"Me too."

Your child needs to learn that behavioral expectations vary in different environments. He will learn at an early age to determine what behaviors work with mother or father and what behaviors are effective with grandparents. Your child has the ability to live in two homes and with two sets of standards. As a 10-year-old said, "Life is a trade-off; you never have everything." If you provide consistency in your home, your child will be able to adapt to different expectations in other environments and to be successful in them.

Use rules to guide discipline.⁵

Single parenting needs to be founded on a sensible system of family discipline and house rules. Too little discipline, and your child will be occupied with the task of testing the limits. Too much discipline will stifle her creatively and socially and may cause rebellion down the road.

Make a list of rules. Prioritize your list by putting the most important items first. Select 3-5 of the most essential rules as your focus. Phrase rules as positively as possible. ("Respect the property of others" is positive. "Do not touch anyone else's property" is negative.) Make a list of consequences for breaking the rules. For example,

- *Give one warning.* The warning should hold your child responsible for her behavior. Simply say, "What are you doing?" This question encourages introspection. Your child is forced to look at her responsibility in the behavior. Asking "What is the rule?" enforces the rule while giving her the opportunity to think that she is making a choice, in this case, a bad choice. If your child changes her choice from a bad choice to a good choice, you have held her responsible for her own behavior—which is the only effective way to change behavior.⁶

- *If the behavior continues, implement a time-out.* Remove your child from the situation. Time-out may be in a chair in her room. If you are in the car, it may mean just a few minutes of silence. If you are in the mall, you may need to stop shopping for a few minutes and go to a quiet area with your child. Optimal time-out is 3-5 minutes. One way to determine the length of time-out is 1 minute per year of age. So, a 4-year-old would get 4 minutes.

- *Have your child face the consequences of her decision or choice to break the rule.* Try to use logical consequences, such as cleaning up if she makes a mess or a period of time-out if she loses control.

(25) What is the best way for me to discipline my child?

Discipline is the guidance of your child toward self-control. Discipline does not mean punishment. The key to successful discipline is establishing rules and rewards for following rules. You do not want to bribe your child to behave, but you do want to let him reap the rewards for making good choices. Discipline provides guidance towards making good choices.

(26) What is the most important goal of disciplining my child?

The goal of discipline is to teach your child how to make good choices. Discipline fosters independence and competence and helps her develop self-control.

(27) What should I do when my child challenges the rules?

Enforce the consequences you have outlined. They are fair, reasonable, and based on reality. They are logical consequences in line with the offense. Just enforce them, hold your ground, and let the pieces fall where they may. Your child needs the security of knowing there are limits.

(28) How will my child test my limits?

Your child may test your limits by directly challenging your authority, begging until you give in, breaking the rules to see if you are serious, and sneaking around and getting revenge if she is disciplined. You are ahead of the game if you have preestablished rules and consequences. Your child will learn where the limits are and will not need to test them continuously.

(29) How do I establish house rules for my child?

Have a family meeting to discuss the rules, rewards, and consequences. Let everyone share ideas for rules. Write down every idea, and then select about 3 rules to emphasize. Allow your child to be involved in selecting positive rewards and negative consequences. Post a list as a reminder.

(30) How can I enforce house rules I have made with my child?

A system of consequences based on reality is the most effective enforcement of house rules. Positive praise and encouragement are the most effective rewards for positive behaviors. Allow your child to earn stars on a chart that shows his progress. If you elect to use points towards a treat or shared activity, be sure you can deliver. If money or time prevents you from giving earned rewards, they lose their power. Establish realistic consequences. Be able to supervise time-out or loss of TV privileges, or your child will learn there are no consequences for bad choices.

(31) How can I teach my child that loving her doesn't mean permissiveness?

Teach values from early on. For example, say: "Too much candy makes you sick. I want you to have good health, and too much sugar will keep you from having good health"; or "Your friend drives too fast, so I can't let you ride with him because he might have an accident." Tell the story of the little girl in your class whose parents spoiled and indulged her. She always had candy at school and had bakery sweets, cupcakes, and cookies for snacks. When she grew up, she became obese and developed health problems. Her parents were too permissive, and her health was the price. Your child will come to understand that rules are for her safety and sometimes may mean not being able to do what she wants to do.

(32) How may overly strict parenting affect my child?

Overly strict or authoritarian parenting uses rewards and punishments in order to control behavior. An authoritarian parent values obedience and tends to be harsh. This type of parenting will rob your child of self-esteem and independence by indicating that authority means power. He will have no freedom and will not learn to make decisions.[5]

(33) How may permissive parenting affect my child?

Permissive parenting puts your child in control. She needs the security of parental limits. She will keep pushing until she finds limits. Permissive parenting robs your child of self-respect and self-esteem because you do things for her that she could do for herself. This is also an invitation to rebellion.[6]

Instead of permissive parenting, use authoritative parenting. It respects your child's abilities but also establishes a standard of behavior. An authoritative parent is both warm and demanding.

Consult experts.

The major role of the family is to help your child meet his full potential. The family must provide for all his needs. As he grows older, the family will allow him to become more independent. With family change, family members support each other as they cope with the stress of change. If your family has difficulty coping with this stress, or if your attempts to develop self-discipline in your child fail, and you feel out of control or inadequate, get help from a school or church counselor. Seek expert advice from trusted relatives, friends, a minister, or your family physician. Family counseling services may be necessary to help your family over the rough spots.

(34) How can an expert help me and my other children understand the difficulty one child may be experiencing from the loss of a parent?

If one child is having more difficulty than the others when a parent moves out, ask a counselor or a minister to spend special time talking and working with that child. A counselor can help you understand the child's problems and can also talk with your other children as a family. It isn't necessary to violate one child's privacy in order to discuss problems with the others. You can give them general information such as, "Jim is having a really hard time since Mom left. We need to give him special attention until he can feel better about things. He will see Mr. Reeds at church to talk on Wednesdays until he feels okay."

(35) What advice from experts can help me with the demands of single parenting?

Because you do not have enough time to go around, it is easy to get busy and push your child aside in order to do housework, errands, and chores. However, because she has suffered the loss of a parent, she needs time and love even more than a child with two parents. Reassure your child that she is secure and an important part of your life. Love her through the hard times as she has loved you through your hard times.

Spend quality time with your child.

Time is a limited resource. You have only 24 hours a day to fulfill your multiple roles. Spend quality time with your child while doing other routine activities such as cooking, driving, or shopping. Take advantage of these times to show your interest in your child's life.

(36) How will time spent with my child show her how much I love her?

To a child, shared time equates to love. Spend time with your child. Every time she asks you to do something, write it down on a list. Keep the list all week. Put a check beside the activity she asks for the most. On a good day when you have time to spend, show the list to your child. Tell her that even though you don't have time to do everything she wants to do, it is important to you to spend time together. Let her choose one thing from the list—and then do it! She will know how much you care and will understand that you would spend more time if you could.

(37) How can I provide parenting for my child equal to that in a two-parent home?

You cannot be two parents; it is impossible. Trying to be two parents is frustrating. Do not waste valuable time feeling guilty. As a single parent, you may spend more time interacting with your child without another adult competing for your time.

(38) How can I give my child the parenting time she needs when I don't have enough time to go around?

Do what really counts. With house rules intact, put aside time for your child that is quality rather than disorganized and punitive. When you are in control, you have streamlined your parenting time. Make a list of your 5 most important goals in life. Allot time according to priority. If you have 30 extra minutes a day for parenting (because now you don't have to clean up bedrooms), and you have 2 children, give each child 15 minutes alone with you each day that is their time, uninterrupted. This can go a long way toward establishing self-esteem.

(39) How can I streamline parenting time?

Establishing rules of discipline can make single parenting more efficient, giving you more time to parent because you need less time to attend to crisis after crisis. Changing the rules can be inefficient. You cannot enforce rules one day and not enforce them the next day. Insecurity will develop, and your child will be constantly asking for guidance so that he will know the limits. This can be very time-consuming. The most efficient timesaver for you is a set of clear, enforceable rules that guide your child and give you the ability to spend your time in an effective manner.

(40) How can I prioritize my time with my child?

First, meet physical needs (food and shelter). Engage in productive work that provides financially for your child. Second, provide safety and security. You develop his sense of safety and security in the environment through your love and consistency in meeting his needs. Once the needs of safety and security are met, a sense of belonging results.

(41) What is the most important energy I can expend as a parent?

Focus your energy on enjoying your role as a parent. Spend fun time with your child. Turn chores into a game. Play music as you do chores. Let her share her feelings as you clean the kitchen together.

(42) If I have more more than one child, how can I meet all of their needs?

You can't meet all of your children's needs, but you can try to meet the important ones. Think of your children one at a time; analyze their needs. Remember that feeling secure and loved are universal needs. You don't need to spend equal time with each child; rather, allot your time to meet specific needs. Do not feel guilty about time you don't have.

(43) If I have more than one child, should their ages affect how I prioritize the time I spend with them?

Any age, depending on individual differences, can be the most sensitive. Your toddler or preschooler will express more immediate fears. Just because your older child doesn't communicate as much does not mean he needs less support. He needs his equal share, though perhaps in different ways.

(44) Will my child need more parenting time at different ages?

When you become a parent, there is no course to teach you what to do. There are no instructions. You do not have to qualify for a license to parent. There is no warranty on children. They were not made to order. You parent a child according to her needs, not yours. Parenting is a selfless job. In order to know how much support your child needs, pay attention to her behavior. The amount of parenting time needed may increase as she faces different stresses such as illness, school problems, or insecurities. Your attention can give her the strength to meet these challenges.

(45) Does my older child need less parenting time than my younger child?

Teenagers report wanting more adult attention and guidance. So even though your older child may demand independence, he really wants and needs your time and love as he grows and changes. He needs your time just as much as your younger child, just in a different way.

(46) How can I balance my work demands and my time with my child?

Avoid bringing work home with you. If you need to do extra work, go in early and get it done quickly instead of mixing it with your important parenting and family time. If your problems are lessened with more effective parenting, you may not feel the need to spend time during the workday lingering over coffee and complaining to co-workers, which is a real timewaster. You can be on the road to confidence, efficiency, and success in both realms. Remember, if you complain at work about too many problems at home, you may be overlooked for important advances at work that could help you financially.

(47) Considering my time limitations, should I volunteer in my child's school?

Showing interest in your child's school is very important. If the school knows you are interested in your child, the school will be interested in her. But your time is precious, and there is too little of it, so think of creative ways to volunteer that will not take a great deal of time. Contribute materials or participate in a phone chain, things that will not require time away from work but would make your presence felt.

(48) Considering my time limitations, should I volunteer in the community?

Make every second of your time count. Volunteer behavior reaps many rewards for your child and for your status as a single-parent family. Engage in volunteer activities that can be enjoyed as a family while providing a service for those in need. Time spent helping others provides a boost in your emotional development, which also benefits your family.

Conclusion

All children are different. Understanding developmental differences can help you provide appropriate environments and interactions to nurture the growth of your child and to help him adjust to family changes. Use positive parenting strategies such as encouraging age-appropriate behavior, focusing on the positive, being consistent, enforcing rules to guide discipline, consulting expert advice when needed, and spending quality time with your child.

The chapters that follow apply these strategies to each stage of childhood growth and development. They include specific suggestions at each stage to support you as a single parent in your multiple roles.

Notes

[1]Jean Piaget and Barbara Inhelder, *Psychology of the Child* (New York: Basic Books, Harper Collins, 1969).

[2]Lev Semenovich, *The Collected Works of L. S. Vygotsky*, trans. Rieber and Carton (New York: Plenum, 1987).

[3]Kevin Leman, *Bringing Kids Up Without Tearing Them Down* (Nashville: Nelson Publishers, 1995).

[4]Lois Hoffman, *Review of the Research* (Ann Arbor MI: University of Michigan, 1984).

[5]Kevin Leman, *Making Children Mind Without Losing Yours* (New York: Dell Publishers, 1984).

[6]William L. Glasser, *Schools Without Failure* (New York: Harper & Row, 1969).

Infants

In the birthing room, the mother looked over to see her new infant. Her first thought was, even though this was a girl, she looked exactly like her brother who was now 3. There could be no mistaking this child for someone else's, thought the mother. The genetic blueprint was exact. The delivering physician marveled; she also had delivered the older child. The power of heredity held onlookers in awe. How could any phenomenon be so powerful as to produce a nearly-exact replica 3 years later? For the first year, the family always dressed the infant in pink so that one day in the future a delineation could be made between the two infants in the family photo album.

The birth of a baby is a spectacular event. It signals a new era in the life of a family. Infants are completely dependent on adults to meet their needs. They need to be fed when they're hungry. They need to be changed when they're soiled. They need to be held and loved and rocked. Infants' needs must come first since they cannot do anything for themselves. In return for care, parents receive emotional fulfillment.

New parents experience a flood of feelings. They may feel overwhelmed with the responsibility that lies ahead, but will develop a unique relationship with this new person who will give unqualified love and absolute trust. Through the eyes of an infant, parents will rediscover childhood pleasures. They will experience the pride and joy, love and exhilaration of parenthood. They will give unconditional love, instill values and traditions, establish a high self-esteem, and teach through example. This is a wonderful experience, but a tall order for two people. It appears to be an insurmountable and exhausting experience for a single parent. How can one parent alone rise to this monumental task?

Recognize signs
of grief and stress.

The birth of an infant should be a time of happiness and comfort, but for a single parent, it can be a time of crisis. If you are not a single parent by choice, you may not be prepared to deal with the emotional trauma of the loss of a partner at a time when you feel a strong need to be united with another parent. Even those who have chosen to be single parents will feel a void. This can be a time of stress that will challenge your emotional and physical strength. The positive side of parenting may seem obscure to you because of the loss of your partner.

Your infant may also experience anxiety and adjustment problems in response to your behavior. Do not let these stresses rob you of the joy of watching your baby develop each day. Find ways to gain emotional support.

(49) What feelings will I experience as I mourn the loss of my partner?

Mourning any loss is similar to mourning the death of a loved one. As a result of her work regarding death and dying, Elizabeth Kübler Ross outlined 5 stages of grief: denial, anger, disbelief, shock, and acceptance.[1] You can get stuck in any one of these stages. If this happens to you, you may not know what is making you miserable, but you do know you are not happy. A minister or a counselor can help you through these stages.

(50) What will happen if I can't get past the stage of anger?

It is common to get stuck in the stage of anger. Anger can consume you. If you are harboring resentments, you cannot offer emotional support to your infant. It is necessary to get to the stage of acceptance, and this takes time. Your efforts to understand your needs strengthen you. Either you get better, or you get bitter. Focus on letting go of the anger and getting on with your life. This may be a good time to join a support group or to read a self-help book.

(51) How can I finally reach the stage of acceptance?

Take one step at a time. As you were growing up, you sometimes imagined the family you would have in the future. This vision was fueled by television and magazines. It usually included two parents in a fairy tale relationship—"They lived happily ever after." Whether you are a single parent by choice or because of death or divorce or separation, you will mourn the loss of this fairy tale image. This sense of loss can be enhanced by visions of other families in the maternity ward who appear to have everything. You need to enlist outside support to help you move forward.

(52) Does my infant know if there is strife in the home?

Your infant will feel the tension when there are problems between his parents. Although he does not have the cognitive skills to understand the problem, he will respond to the environment. Your infant's needs for nurturing cannot be met when his parents are focusing their energy on disagreements.

(53) Does my infant know when I am stressed?

Your infant will be very aware of your emotional state. She may respond to your moods. Your depression or stress can limit the energy available to nurture and stimulate her.

(54) How will stress and/or loss affect my infant?

When your infant is exposed to stress, feeding and sleeping problems can result. He may become fussy and cause extra stress. If he is too quiet, he may also be reacting to stress.

(55) Should I tend to my infant each time he shows signs of distress?

Your infant needs emotional comfort during times of stress. Also, your dependability in meeting his physical needs is an important part of the learning process for him. He needs to learn to trust his caregivers and environment to meet his needs. Building this sense of trust is an essential task during infancy. It provides the basis for future development.

(56) How can I care for my infant when I am feeling stressed?

Find creative ways to care for your infant. Use a bottle holder at feeding time. Use a mechanical swing to calm him to sleep. Install a jumping seat in a doorway to help him with entertainment and exercise. Allow an older infant to follow you around the house in a walker. These substitutes are not better than being rocked or held by a loving person, but they work.

(57) What should I do if I cannot deal with my own grief and thus spend the quality time I desire with my infant?

If you feel too upset to have calm time with your infant, it may be better to do something that will develop a future benefit, such as taking a part-time job until you are able to feel more settled or stable. Going back to school for completion of a degree may be a satisfying emotional and financial step. Good child care at this point will benefit both you and your infant. The best solution is a grandparent who is retired and has the time and love to give. Child care in your home may be the easiest approach but may not be in your budget. Family day care, with a limited number of children, may be an option. Commercial daycare may also provide good care.

(58) How will the loss of a parent affect my infant in the 7-12 month age range?

If the absent parent leaves the household when your child is an older infant, it can cause great distress. Between the ages of 7 and 12 months, your infant will begin to respond to the passage of time. She may look for a working parent to appear at a certain time or may become stressed at variations in schedules. She can sense change but is unable to verbalize her concern. The symptoms of distress may be most observable at times when she regularly had contact with the absent parent, for instance, at bath time.

(59) How can I help my older infant deal with separation anxiety?

Separation anxiety is normal for the 7-12 month age range and may increase following the loss of a parent. It is normal for your infant to cling and exhibit signs of frustration when you are out of sight. Since this is the age when anger, night frights, and tantrums emerge, your guilt can be aggravated when you have to be away.

Your infant needs to feel trust in her environment. She needs to know you'll be there as expected. Therefore, try to avoid extended separation. Verbally reassure your infant you will return. When you leave, do not leave while she is asleep unless you know you will return before she awakes. Take the time to tell her you are leaving but will return. Do not show your anxiety.

The symptoms of distress will be less intense if your infant receives a lot of attention to help meet her needs for close relationships. This attention can come from other family members and trusted sitters as well as the custodial parent.

Ask for help.

Your infant cannot initially discriminate among people. As long as his needs are met, he is physically satisfied. He is emotionally satisfied when he is held or stroked. He enjoys being talked to when he is happy. This interaction provides social satisfaction for caregivers. Parents of multiples (twins or triplets) enlist friends and neighbors to help in nurturing their infants. You, too, need to enlist others to help.

(60) Should I spend time with my infant if I am really stressed out?

If there are other caring adults who can give time to your infant, they may provide soothing care when you are too anxious. When you are more relaxed, take time to provide the eye contact, stroking, rocking, and singing that can help you and your infant grow closer. Use swings, strollers, music, mobiles, and teddy bears to soothe her when you are stressed. Do not waste time feeling guilty.

Take advantage of Mothers Morning Out or other programs where you may safely leave your infant for short periods of time on a regular basis. Many churches sponsor these programs. A child in the neighborhood may want to play with your infant to give you time out to rest or work in another room of the house.

(61) Is it better to let a family member take over caring for my infant for a time?

If you are upset, allow a sister, brother, or grandparent to take over until things settle down. Everyone needs some time out. If the time away from your infant contributes to your emotional well-being, you will be a better parent later. Focus on meeting your needs so that you can meet your infant's needs.

(62) How can I get enough rest?

Sleep deprivation can increase your stress levels. You need rest. Ask family members or friends to help with your child and the housework. Practice stress reduction techniques such as relaxation and deep breathing. Talk with someone who can understand your stress. Also consult your doctor about diet and exercise.

(63) What should I do if I feel exhausted?

Symptoms of exhaustion after childbirth or hormonal adjustment problems from mood swings due to postpartum depression are normal. Discuss these problems with your obstetrician. Give attention to good health habits such as exercise and a proper diet. Relaxation strategies can also be helpful.

(64) How can I be an effective parent if I am a "nervous wreck"?

All parents of infants suffer symptoms of stress. The disruption of sleep patterns is a major contributor to this stress. Lack of sleep can make you a nervous wreck. If you are anxious, your infant will become anxious along with you. You may need some time to calm down. If outside help can be consistent and calm, it may be best to have another person provide the majority of the care under your supervision until you are in control of calmer emotions.

(65) Does my infant know if I am not there to take care of him?

As long as there is a loving caretaker to meet his needs, your infant can be content. Don't feel guilty about not being the primary caregiver. Parents in some cultures have traditionally turned their children over to nannies or other caregivers. Your ability to develop an emotional bond with your infant may be increased if you have support in meeting his needs.

(66) How can I cope with the enormous task of parenting my infant alone?

Don't try to handle all parenting tasks alone. This is no time to let your pride or independence rule. Post a schedule of chores, and get others to participate. If you have no friends or family available, try community agencies. There are many people willing to volunteer to help. Contact a local church or United Way for assistance. It is okay to let others share in the parenting of your infant.

Provide a stimulating environment.

Your infant needs experiences full of color, sound, and movement. She requires much stimulation to develop readiness for later learning. Plan some active play time with your infant when you are both feeling rested and happy. Ask your parents or other relatives and friends to spend some active play time with her as well.

(67) What can I do to bond with my infant?

Play with your infant. Feed him. Sing to him. Talk to him. Give him loving hugs and kisses. Play with him at a time when you feel in control of your life and emotions. The quality of the time you share is more important than the quantity of the time you share.

(68) What are some ways I can play with my infant?

Your infant needs different types of stimulation such as that received from singing, storytelling, playing simple games, and active or rowdy play.

(69) What should I do if the absent parent is unavailable to play with my infant?

If one parent is unavailable, then enlist a friend or family member to provide more active play or to sing and nurture as is needed. Older siblings can provide excellent support, even though they need supervision when they play with their infant sibling.

(70) Is it better for my infant to stay at home?

Consult with your pediatrician to determine when your infant is ready for excursions. If there are no medical reasons for staying at home, being around other people can be beneficial to your infant and can also provide comfort to you. The noise and bustle of the outside world is stimulating to her. A walk in a stroller or shopping cart or a ride in the infant seat in the car can soothe her when she's fussy. Before scheduling trips, consider your infant's schedule. Decide if you will need to focus on her during excursions or if you want to go during her nap time.

(71) Should I limit the number of people who come in contact with my infant?

It is better to have more people around your infant. He will learn to interact with others, and you will benefit from the compliments of adoring passersby. Isolating yourself may create more stress. Excursions relieve the sense of isolation you may feel as a single parent. Inviting friends and neighbors to drop by can help. Strolling your infant through the neighborhood may provide the opportunity to meet other parents, perhaps even some having experiences similar to yours.

Introduce new people gradually.

As your infant matures, she will begin to discriminate among people and develop stranger anxiety. This is a normal stage of development. She will cling to the mother or scream in fear. Other persons, including the absent parent or grandparents, have to be presented slowly and calmly before active play can begin. This can be very stressful for parents absent from the home. It can also develop if a parent must travel for work.

(72) What is a preferable visitation schedule for my infant?

Your infant will benefit more from short, frequent visits rather than longer, less frequent visits. Sometimes this is not possible, and you must use creative strategies to bridge the gap.

(73) What can I do to bridge the gap between my infant and the absent parent?

Place a special toy or object from the absent parent in the crib. Even a worn t-shirt belonging to the absent parent can help establish a multisensory presence of the absent parent. Show your infant pictures of the absent parent, and talk about the parent. No matter what your relationship is with the absent parent, your infant needs to feel secure in the love of both parents and shouldn't be exposed to bad feelings.

(74) Will my infant sustain a relationship with the absent parent?

It is difficult for your infant to sustain a relationship with someone she does not see often. She does not have the skills to remember people over a period of time. She may react to the absent parent as if that person were a stranger. The absent parent may feel rejected. The key to maintaining the relationship is to provide some consistency, such as a familiar environment. If your infant senses stress in either the custodial parent or absent parent, she will react. Soothing words and actions will help her calm herself.

(75) Will my infant accept the absent parent if that parent is not present on a regular basis?

Whether your infant accepts the absent parent will depend on her developmental stage and also the love, care, and concern the absent parent shows for her during visits. Visitation time should focus on your infant. If possible, both parents may spend some time together with her to help ease the transition. The absent parent will also need time alone with her to establish a relationship.

(76) What can I do to help the absent parent bond with my infant?

Encourage the other parent to read a nursery rhyme or story or sing a song on tape. Place pictures of the absent parent in the nursery and regularly introduce the pictures. Create a familiar presence with a t-shirt that carries the absent parent's scent.

(77) How can a tape recording help my infant bond with the absent parent?

A tape recording can help establish the absent parent as a presence in your infant's life and can help prevent difficult scenes when that parent visits. If the absent parent does not make frequent contact, the familiar voice will reduce anxiety for your infant when the parent does visit. The ritual of listening to the tape also helps establish an emotional bond. Preparing the tape provides an opportunity for the absent parent to actively parent.

Look for developmental milestones.

Your infant will undergo dramatic transformations during the first year of life. From a helpless newborn, he will prepare to enter the age of a toddler. There are some milestones along the way that will allow you to monitor his progress. The time and order of each milestone will vary between infants, but in general, the developmental milestones are indicators of normal progress. These are general guides for pediatricians and parents; there are no rigid standards.

(78) What are the developmental milestones for my infant?

Generally, during your infant's first year, she will develop skills according to the following guidelines:[2]

- *2nd month*—smile, startle reflex spontaneously, hold head up for a short time, hold or swipe at objects, stare at surroundings, track objects visually, show delight and distress, smile at family members, follow a moving person visually
- *3rd month*—play with toys, sit supported, coo, follow objects with eyes, reach for objects, study human faces, turn head to speaking voices, vocalize when talked to, grasp objects
- *4th month*—turn head in all directions, pull to stand by parent, reach with arms, babble, react to tickle, vocalize mood, discriminate among faces
- *5th month*—sit alone, show fear and anger, recognize familiar objects, reach with two hands, visually search or track, imitate sounds and movements, cry when left by a parent
- *6th month*—sit alone, interact with family
- *7th month*—crawl, self-feed
- *8th month*—react to strangers, grasp objects, pull to stand
- *9th month*—react to siblings
- *10th month*—look for social approval, remember people and faces
- *11th month*—stand alone, attempt to walk, test limits
- *12th month*—walk, talk, explore environment

This is only a general guide of some of the stages to expect. Child development books can give you complete information on these various milestones of infancy.

(79) What are language milestones for my infant?

Language developmental milestones include babbling, turning in the direction of sound, and smiling in response to familiar voices. Verbal stimulation is essential to the development of these skills. Your infant is never too young for someone to read to her. Singing, imitating animal noises, and reciting nursery rhymes also provide stimulation.

(80) What are vision milestones for my infant?

Developmental milestones for vision are following moving objects, recognizing faces or familiar objects, using eyes and hands in coordination, and watching familiar facial expressions. You can provide developmentally appropriate toys (check the label on the toy box for guidelines) to stimulate the development of your infant's skills. Less expensive options may be used as long as you check for safety (size, shapes, edges, etc.). Visual stimulation can be provided by large black and white pictures at first. More colorful pictures can be introduced as your infant begins to differentiate colors.

(81) What are social milestones for my infant?

Social developmental milestones include smiling, playing, crying, using facial expressions, and imitating movements. You can help your infant master these developmental milestones by providing social stimulation and opportunities for these skills to develop.

(82) What are movement milestones for my infant?

Developmental milestones for movement are raising the head and chest when lying on the stomach, stretching the legs and kicking when lying on the back, opening and shutting hands, pushing down on the feet when placed on a surface, bringing hands to the mouth, grasping and shaking toys, and hitting at dangling toys or familiar objects. Infant motor development moves from the head down.

At birth, your infant needs support for his head since his neck muscles are not strong enough. As his motor skills improve, he will begin to support his head by himself. Large motor skills, such as moving arms, develop before fine motor skills, such as grasping objects. Fun activities stimulate motor development, for instance, moving his arms for "pat-a-cake" and "bicycle wheels."

(83) What should be my main priorities in raising my infant?

The results of your time and effort should produce a confident, secure infant with high self-esteem. She should feel loved and needed. If she feels worthwhile and important, she will be ready for the next stage of development and new developmental milestones.

Conclusion

The joy of the birth of a baby is a wonderful experience. It also represents the beginning of a lifelong challenge. The physical and emotional stress on you may be compounded by the grief experienced due to the separation from or absence of one parent. Your main priority is to be dependable in meeting your infant's needs and providing lots of love and nurturing. Understanding developmental milestones will help you provide appropriate interactions.

Dependability in making sure your infant's needs are met is important, but you don't have to do it alone. Learn to ask for help from relatives and friends. You can't meet your infant's needs when you are exhausted and stressed out. First, meet your own needs. Your proper nutrition, exercise, and rest will benefit everyone. Then you will have the energy to spend more quality time to bond with your infant. Involving others also limits your sense of isolation. Introduce new people gradually so that your infant will not be frightened. Involve the absent parent in his life as much as possible.

Notes

[1] Elisabeth Kübler-Ross and Barbara Inheldar, *On Death and Dying* (New York: Basic Books, HarperCollins, 1969).

[2] Frank D. Caplan, *The First Twelve Months of Life* (New York: Perigree Books, 1993).

Toddlers

"Baby Soup!" cried the toddler. By now she was soaked in tears and perspiration. She had drooled all over her new dress and was crying upside down as she balanced with her head and feet on the floor. She was bent over at the waist, which made her tears go up instead of down, soaking her hair. The tears were flowing. The toddler was near hysteria. With renewed screams of rage, she tugged on her dress in frustration, desperately trying to get it off.

Her mother was busy trying to open a can of Campbell's™ soup, the kind with ABC's in it, in an attempt to satisfy the toddler's demands for "Baby Soup." When the toddler looked into the can of soup, however, she squealed in renewed frustration, shaking her head back and forth in a dramatic "NO!" The mother then opened tomato soup, thinking that might be the magic soup. It was not.

The toddler ran out of the kitchen into the carpeted area and fell on the floor limp with exhaustion. This tantrum had gone on for more than an hour, and this was the fourth kind of soup the mother had offered in vain. The frustrated but sympathetic mother took a favorite blanket, a bottle of juice, and a special pillow to the toddler who was wracked in sobs that shook her whole body. The mother prayed the toddler would just fall asleep.

Quieted in the sympathy of her mother, and understanding the "I'm sorry I don't know what you want. You get it yourself if you can. You get Baby Soup," the toddler resolutely went into her room, blinked back tears, and tediously began to open drawers in search of "Baby Soup."

Thirty silent minutes passed, but contented in the proactive pursuit of her desires, the toddler made slow, steady headway. She finally emerged in a red two-piece bikini with white polka dots. It had ruffles on the bottom and a little ruffle-like skirt on the waistband upside down and backwards. There was a tiny white ribbon on the top slightly off center. The toddler had calmed herself completely and smiled with her two new baby teeth on the bottom center touching the top center baby teeth. She *pointed to her bikini and explained to her exhausted mother, "Dis Baby Soup." Her mother, in an expression of relief, repeated, "Baby Soup, Oh! Baby Suit! Bathing Suit!" The toddler had wanted to go to the beach!*

The toddler gave an intriguing nod of agreement. She was certainly more concerned with directing her world than her limited language skills could ever have indicated! With this new insight into the toddler's world, the mother took care to give her more choices, to include the toddler in simple decision making, and to listen more closely to her ever-growing vocabulary as she tried to attach labels to the world around her.

When infants grow beyond age 1 or 1½, they begin to walk, thus entering the toddler stage of development. Crawling vigorously, walking, and talking are signs of dawning independence. The days of total dependency will soon end. Power struggles are a portent of things to come, and the words "No!" and "Mine!" earmark the toddler stage.

This is a stage of exploring the boundaries of their physical limits as well as testing the limits of rules. Since learning to walk represents their most important developmental milestone at this age, toddlers will be interested in finding out where their footsteps can take them. Curiosity and emerging independence will lead them into new and sometimes dangerous situations. You have to hustle to stay one step ahead of them.

Toddlers will test your will along with their new independence, and they will resort to temper tantrums to assert their will against yours. The toddler creed goes something like this:

> If I see it, it is mine!
> If I have it, it is mine!
> If I ever touched it, it is mine!
> If it looks like mine, it is mine!
> If I like it, it is mine!
> If it is yours and you put it down, it is mine!
> If you have it and I want it, it is mine!

Toddlers can be very possessive. They will resort to physical aggression in order to keep possessions they consider "mine." They will engage in a tug of war with other children and may hit or kick for possession of things they want. They may fight for things only to reject them unexpectedly when they win them.

Although speech skills are limited at this time, toddlers are able to understand much of what you say to them. They use telegraphic speech to express themselves. It is very short and to the point, such as "Baby Soup!" for "I want to go to the beach and wear my red polka dot bathing suit with the ruffles on it." Toddlers need to hear short, simple sentences such as, "Give me the ball," or "Put the blocks here." Their limited language skills often lead to frustration and tantrums.

Develop receptive language ability.

Receptive language is the first step in the development of comprehension skills. Your toddler will suddenly seem to understand everything you say. If you mention you are going to the store, he will go to the closet for a coat or shoes so that he can join you. All at once, he understands your words, and you must screen what you say in his presence. This is the stage when many parents begin to spell out words they don't want toddlers to take into their vocabulary.

(84) How can I enhance my toddler's language skills?

Talk to your toddler. She will be responsive to adult conversation and will even contribute in a limited way. By talking to her, you help her develop good language so that she can learn to communicate. Give directions in short simple sentences. Elaborate on her answer by rephrasing it as a short sentence. For example,

Parent: "Put the toy away."
Toddler: "Toy?"
Parent: "That's right. Put the toy away."

(85) How can I help my toddler develop a good vocabulary?

Playing naming games can help your toddler develop a good vocabulary. You can do this while driving or doing something else. Nouns or naming words are the first words toddlers use. Naming pictures in books and magazines is fun. Animals and animal sounds, nonsense verses, and picture books provide opportunities for imagination and memorization.

(86) What types of books should I read to my toddler?

Your toddler will develop language at a rapid pace, so you don't want to limit reading to naming books only. Reading aloud fairy tales and classic books such as *Dr. Seuss.* will benefit your toddler's language acquisition and help him with proper sentence structure, as well as expanding his vocabulary. Always read books with more complex language than he speaks, since receptive language exceeds expressive language (he understands more than he can say). Your toddler's memory will amaze you. If you paraphrase or change a word in a favorite story, he will correct you.

(87) What are some games I can play with my toddler?

Your toddler will enjoy playing "peek-a-boo" and searching for hidden objects. (She has moved from the "out of sight, out of mind" stage into the stage of object constancy.) She is proud of her knowledge that even though you cannot always see something, it still exists. Games of tag can make her squeal with laughter. "Hide-and-seek" is a thrilling game. "Pat-a-cake" and other rhythmic games provide the bonus of establishing motor skills. Talking about the game helps develop language skills, for instance, "Where did it go? It is under the blanket."

(88) Should I play make-believe with my toddler?

Pretending is a significant part of your toddler's developmental stage. He does not separate fact from fantasy. If something exists in his mind, it exists. Playing make-believe with your toddler provides him with the opportunity for role recognition. It helps him make sense of the world around him. He may wear your hat and pretend to be you. He may pretend to drive, eat, or run. He may pretend to be a bird, a dog, or a cat. Talking about the make-believe activities helps develop language skills, for example, say, "I can go bow-wow like a dog."

Develop expressive language ability.

By 18 months, your toddler will be able to tell you some of her needs and will have an expressive vocabulary of 10-20 words. She will be learning complex language skills. Often she will use 2 words to express a complete thought. It may be difficult to know exactly what she means. For example, "Dog go" could mean "The dog is going away," or "Put the dog outside." Between 18 months and 3 years, your toddler will gradually improve in her expression. She will begin to link several words together and form simple sentences. At first, she will use mostly nouns (naming words) and verbs (action words). By the time she reaches the age of 3, she will have acquired an average vocabulary of several hundred words.

(89) How can I encourage my toddler's expressive vocabulary?

Avoid baby talk, for it provides an inappropriate language model. Avoid discussing things in detail, for your toddler will feel over-loaded and tune you out. Listen to song tapes and sing along. Watch educational television programs developed for his age group. Watch for shows or videos that encourage viewers to sing along or respond verbally. Show interest in your toddler's verbalizations. Repeat his phrases.

(90) How can I expand my toddler's expressive language?

Encourage your toddler to respond verbally. Don't ask yes or no questions. Give her something to imitate. For example,

Parent: "What do you want for lunch?"
Toddler: "Peanut butter."
Parent: "You want a peanut butter sandwich?'
Toddler: "Yes."
Parent: "Say the whole thing: I want a peanut butter sandwich."

(91) How can I understand my toddler's speech?

Your toddler's limited speech can lead to frustration when you do not understand what she is trying to say. She may gesture wildly, making sounds that imitate adult language, but without the structure. There are so many challenges, she can become overwhelmed. Tantrums are common reactions and can lead to frustration for you. Your toddler will also become frustrated at your inability to understand her. Show interest in her. Try to pick out a key word to repeat. Ask her to show you what she wants.

(92) Should I allow my toddler to watch television?

Because your toddler is unable to discern fact from fantasy, he will accept anything on television as reality. If he can imagine it, it is real. For this reason, it is important to screen all television programs. Teaching programs such as "Shari Lewis," "Sesame Street," "Mr. Rogers," or "Barney" can provide good stimulation for your toddler. He will learn letters, colors, shapes, sizes, and number concepts by watching Big Bird and other lovable characters.

Accept inconsistent emotions and behavior as normal.

Your **toddler will** display inconsistent emotions that reflect her struggle between her need for parental support and her emerging need for independence. She will also experience many frustrations because her language and motor skill limitations block her attempts at mastering her environment. Adult logic cannot be applied to the actions and reactions of your toddler. She is driven by the here and now. She doesn't remember yesterday's results, and can't understand tomorrow's goals.

Her fierce independence can manifest itself in foot-stomping, screaming, falling on the floor, kicking, head-banging, and general fits of rage and frustration. She cannot explain her feelings. Therefore, increased aggression is a way of letting you know that she is angry. Because she believes you are all powerful, she is angry at you.

Your toddler's displays of anger and frustration may create feelings of guilt for the custodial parent or absent parent. The emotions she expresses may be more difficult for the custodial parent who experiences them constantly. They are also difficult for the absent parent because they appear to be signs of rejection.

(93) How does my toddler view the world?

Your toddler is egocentric. He understands events through his own reactions to them. He also believes in the power of "wishes." He may chant: "Now, now, now" as he waits for cookies to bake. In his view, his chants control the time. When his environment does not respond as he wishes, your toddler may resort to acting-out behavior.

(94) How should I manage my toddler's acting-out behavior?

The best way to manage acting-out behaviors is to allow expressions of anger within limits—your toddler cannot kick, hit, bite others, or damage property. Ignore the behavior when possible. Wait for more acceptable behavior, and then give him attention. Remove him from the cause of frustration. Redirecting him to another activity may stop the behavior. If the behavior is out of control, acknowledge his anger verbally: "I know you feel angry. It's okay to feel angry. When I feel angry, I hit a pillow." Give him the assurance that you are still in charge. It may be necessary to hold him until the anger ceases.

(95) How can I reassure my toddler of my love?

Verbal and physical reassurance of your love and acceptance will help your toddler. Approval or disapproval of specific behaviors must be separated from your love for her. For example, say, "I love you, but hitting is bad. Don't hit!" Physical contact such as holding, hugging, or patting also shows your love.

Provide a safe environment.

Your toddler needs to explore and satisfy his great curiosity. Setting and enforcing limits will be easier if you remove temptations. Put your prized possessions away for a while until they can be safely displayed. Child-proof the house to keep it as safe as possible. Although there are many cabinets you need to lock, there are some that can provide an endless source of joy, such as the cabinet containing pots and pans. Wooden spoons can be added to this cabinet. So, although many places are off-limits, there are places your toddler can explore and learn.

(96) How can I child-proof my toddler's surroundings?

Child-proofing begins with security measures. To prevent exploration into dangerous places, place plastic covers on electrical outlets and locks on cabinets for medicine and toxic cleaning agents. Install baby gates to restrict movement throughout the house or near stairwells. Remove your treasures until your toddler develops self-control.

(97) Should I move everything out of my toddler's reach?

How much you remove from your toddler's reach is a personal decision. Remember, she doesn't have the self-control to avoid temptation. At this age, if it *feels* good, it *is* good. Your toddler's goals are to satisfy her needs. An investment of time to move and protect treasures prevents you from monitoring her at all times. You can remove everything at first and then replace things as she develops self-control later.

(98) How can I be sure my toddler is safe when he leaves my presence to play elsewhere?

Your toddler will begin to play in a different room away from you for short periods of time. This initiates the "life beyond mother" stage of socialization. Having a child-proof house provides you with the assurance that your toddler may play safely out of your sight. You may monitor his activity frequently, but not constantly.

(99) What can I do to keep my toddler safe at the absent parent's home?

Provide outlet covers, locks, and baby gates to ensure safety. Give the parent a pamphlet on child-proofing. Share ideas that work at your home.

(100) Where else should I insist on child-proofing for my toddler?

Give grandparents and sitters outlet covers and other safety devices to use in their homes. Also, make sure places where you visit are safe environments. When you visit friends and neighbors, check for problem areas and ask for permission to set up temporary barriers. For example, put a chair in front of exposed electrical outlets. Focus on your toddler's movement in any new environment in order to protect the possessions of others and to protect the safety of your toddler. He probably won't be a good house guest, but his charm will compensate for some of his driven behavior.

Deal with stress and frustration.

Single parenting is an endless job. Stress can build and cause other problems. Give yourself some reverse time-out. Go to another room or put distance between you and your toddler. If you are driving, pull over and take a deep breath. Stop for gas and a cookie. (Of course, never leave your toddler unattended in a car.) Count to 10 before you act. Put your toddler in a stroller and go for a walk outside. Put yourself back in control of your emotions before you interact with her. Remember, her behavior can change abruptly with a change of scenery or redirection of her activity.

(101) How can I deal with the stress of rearing my toddler alone?

Call on a friend for some help so you can trade off a short period of sitting. Get some exercise. Put your toddler in a stroller and go for a walk. Use relaxation techniques or meditation. Play some calming music. The key is to deal with the stress before it causes problems.

(102) What should I do if I explode and lose my temper with my toddler?

Forgive yourself. No one is perfect. We all have bad days. Then ask your toddler to forgive you. She can learn a valuable lesson from hearing you say: "I'm sorry. It wasn't you; it was me"; or "I was upset about other things, and I yelled at you. I'm sorry." Do not try to win back your toddler's love with bribes; a hug is enough.

(103) What can I do to make up for an occasional outburst to my toddler?

Feeling guilty is a waste of time and energy. Your toddler can withstand an occasional angry outburst from you if he knows he is loved. You don't have to spoil him to compensate. This only sets up future expectations. Simply give him an apology and a hug.

(104) What should I do if angry outbursts become a regular event for me?

If you find yourself constantly overwhelmed and unable to deal with your anger, seek professional help. Occasional outbursts can be related to health issues such as a lack of sleep or exercise or poor eating habits. Personal issues such as anger or guilt can also contribute. Talking about your problems with a professional may help you to identify ways to address the problems. Parenting classes can provide ideas for preventing stressful events. Don't try to be strong and deal with your situation alone. Seeking help is a sign of strength. If you need it, it is the best investment of time and money you can make.

Divert attention before a crisis occurs.

Often you will notice patterns of behavior in your toddler that signal an impending crisis. Remove him from the source of frustration or redirect him to another activity. Give him a hug while he cries. Assure him by your presence that he is safe. Try to avoid angry outbursts, which can be scary for him. He needs to learn other ways to handle the problem.

(105) How should I handle my toddler's tantrums?

Fred was reaching for the racks of candy in the check-out aisle of the grocery store. He was screaming and grabbing candy and gum. He had grabbed several packages while his mother stepped over to pick up a roll of paper towels on an end rack near the buggy. She returned with the paper towels and quietly moved the grocery cart away from the candy. She chose a new aisle that had a longer line but did not have a candy rack. She calmly took the candy away from Fred and asked a store clerk to put it away. She was careful during the next shopping trip to find a check-out aisle without candy racks.

When you are shopping, your options are limited. When you are at home, you can take your toddler to another room and remove her from the object of frustration. A change of scenery will often abruptly end a tantrum.

(106) Should I give in to my toddler's tantrums?

Don't punish your toddler for his tantrums, but at the same time, don't reward him for them. Do not bribe him with food or toys to stop the behavior. You will pay the price for years to come if he learns that tantrums can be used to get what he wants.

(107) Should I leave a business or a restaurant during my toddler's tantrums?

If possible, leave the scene of a tantrum. The busy lives of single parents often make this option an impossible one, however. If you have to complete shopping, ignore the behavior (and the stares of others) and leave as quickly as possible. Meditate on the way home if the tantrum continues. Repeat a phrase such as "I am a good parent, I am a good parent" to keep from losing control. Put your toddler in time-out when you get home and give yourself a reward for keeping calm.

Teach independence.

As your toddler develops more skills, she will be less dependent on you to fulfill all of her needs. She will want to do things herself. This is a good time to channel her energy and desire to imitate adults. Let your toddler help with household chores such as dusting or setting the table. Investing in child-sized versions of cleaning tools is a real motivation. Do not worry about sexual stereotypes at this age.

(108) Should I confine my toddler to a playpen for safety purposes?

Your toddler will quickly get frustrated and begin acting out if he is confined to a playpen. Remember that your goal is to provide freedom to explore and try new things while establishing limits to ensure safety. Your toddler needs freedom to explore in a safe environment. This may take some initial rearranging of the furniture and breakables, but it will benefit his curiosity and need to learn new things. Save the playpen for safety on visits and outings. Fill it with favorite toys to keep your toddler occupied.

(109) Why does my toddler play, return to me, and then go back and play?

You are the safety base for your toddler's explorations of the world around her. She will explore, return to base, explore, and return to base again as she experiences her surroundings. Development at this stage is as varied and diverse as it will be later on in life.

(110) What activities can my toddler do independently?

Fred would take a lick of his ice cream, and the big dog would take a lick. He was careful to feed the dog in equal shares, so whenever it was not Fred's turn, he let the dog have another lick.

Your toddler is able to do a few activities such as feeding and dressing himself, even though he may not do it your way. These are first steps to independence. It takes longer for your toddler to do it alone, and it may be messier, but pride in his effort is worth it.

(111) How will my toddler react to new situations?

Your toddler may react emotionally when she faces new situations. She may cling to you, whine, or have tantrums until she feels comfortable with new people, places, or events. She needs time to adjust. Talk about and/or role-play a new experience with your toddler before leaving a safe, familiar environment or situation for a new experience. Remain present for a while when a new babysitter comes. Remember, your toddler's curiosity to learn and her drive to master her environment can lead to many frustrating experiences.

(112) Why does my toddler have difficulty with new situations?

The toddler stage is often referred to as the first adolescence. The swings in behavior can be frustrating. Your toddler needs the security of a consistent environment. Special problems can occur if you must work unpredictable hours or travel or change residency.

(113) Will my toddler experience independence problems due to one parent leaving the home?

In the attorney's office the mother could hear the screams of fear as the toddler reached for the closed door between the office of the secretary and the office of the attorney. There was no way to solace the toddler who had regressed since the door closed from an adventurous confident toddler to one who could not stand to be out of his mother's sight. His fear escalated as the meeting progressed. After 10 minutes, he was hysterical; the meeting was prematurely adjourned. When the toddler was reunited with his mother, he was a limp, sobbing, soaking wet rag doll. The secretary and the mother exchanged knowing glances.

The fear of loss of parental love is very strong at this stage. Your toddler will fluctuate between independence and dependence, especially when she becomes tired or frustrated. She will transfer the father going away to the mother going away, and will fear losing her, too, or vice versa.

Assist with adjustment following parental separation.

Separation from a parent can create feelings of abandonment and anxiety for your toddler. Because he is very egocentric, he may feel responsible for the separation. The separation may also affect his feelings of trust in his environment. He needs support to deal with his feelings.

(114) How will my toddler react to parental separation?

Your toddler will be deeply affected by family strife. He will worry about what will happen to him when a parent leaves the home. He will miss the family routines and will fear being left out. He may even feel responsible for the separation. However, if you and the other parent are emotionally available despite your own distresses, you can help your toddler develop in healthy ways. He will learn that he can go through difficult times and recover from them.

(115) Since my toddler thinks only in terms of "me," how does the loss of a parent affect her thinking?

Your toddler probably thinks, "If one parent left, the other parent will leave [me], too." She will somehow feel that her behavior is responsible for the separation. This guilt is increased if she has witnessed parental arguments over her behavior. Your toddler's sense of trust may be undermined. Reassure her every day that you will not leave her. Tell her that the absent parent did not leave her, but you.

(116) How does my toddler interpret the fact that Mommy and Daddy don't want to live together?

Your toddler may feel that if Mommy and Daddy leave when they are angry at each other, they may also leave when they are angry at "me." Constantly reassure him this is not true. Tell him that both parents will always love and take care of him. Explain that sometimes grown-ups need to do things they don't like: "We wish we could keep our family together, but it's not possible." Avoid blaming.

(117) What does my toddler understand about one parent moving out?

Your toddler will notice the disruption in her schedules and routines. She will notice the absence of a parent at the table and at family outings. She may harbor secret worries. Both parents should explain the separation to her before it occurs. Keep it simple. Tell your toddler it is not her fault. Tell her where the leaving parent will stay and when that parent will visit. Mark it on the calendar so she can see it.

(118) Should I be more permissive with my toddler after the loss of the other parent?

The most frightening message you can give your toddler is that he is in control. He needs the assurance that you will allow his expressions of emotions, but he needs limits to be set. Permissiveness only confuses him further, making him more insecure. Keeping the rules as consistent as they were before household changes will help your toddler feel safe.

(119) How can I help bridge the gap between my toddler and the absent parent?

Play a tape recording of the absent parent reading a favorite story. A special toy given by the absent parent will reassure your toddler of that parent's love as you show your love with a goodnight kiss. Encourage your toddler to include the absent parent in bedtime prayers. Allow her to take some of her toys to the absent parent's house and to leave them there.

Deal with regressive behavior.

Your toddler will work hard at establishing independence. Sometimes he may feel the need to give up, at least temporarily, and may regress for a period of time back to earlier behaviors. Regressive behavior is normal for a toddler, even in a two-parent home where there is no conflict or stressful change. Regression is especially typical for a toddler who experiences any type of trauma, either physical or emotional.

(120) What are symptoms of regressive behavior in my toddler?

Morris had been potty-trained and had dry nights every night. When he moved to a new house, he began bed-wetting every night. The bed-wetting continued in spite of encouragement and reward charts. It was months later before Morris was able to stop bed-wetting in spite of positive intervention on a regular basis.

Regressive behavior is a return to more dependent behavior typical of younger stages of development. Examples of regressive behavior your toddler may experience include: demanding bottles, bed-wetting, refusing to feed herself, or whining and clinging.

(121) What are some traumas that can cause my toddler to regress?

Exciting, happy events as well as traumatic events can cause your toddler to regress. Planned surgery, an accident requiring hospitalization, the death of a relative, or the birth of a sibling can be sufficient to send him into regressive behavior. A move to a new neighborhood and/or the loss of a parent may also cause regressive behavior.

(122) What does my toddler think when he regresses?

Your toddler learned to trust adults, but the loss of one parent gave him the message that adults cannot be trusted. The distraction of moving and changing family members is difficult. Routines are upset—and your toddler thrives on routines. Regression to old behaviors, which feel safe, gives him time to recover. More dependent behavior also provides the security of more parental contact.

(123) How can I help reestablish my toddler's trust during regression?

Make short-term promises you can keep, such as, "I'll be back in one hour." Then keep those promises. Your toddler has a limited sense of time and needs immediate results. He needs to be able to take you at your word and count on you to do the things you promise so that he can begin to trust again. Set a timer to show when you will return, and then try to return early.

(124) How should I respond to my toddler's regressive behavior?

Accept the regressive behavior while waiting for your toddler's strength and security to return. Be very supportive. He may mistakenly assume that his independence is the cause of the disruption in his home and routine. Gently reassure him to help him move forward again and realize that independence isn't so scary after all. Try saying something like, "You're a big boy now and can use a cup just like me."

(125) Should I be more permissive with my expectations of my toddler during regression?

In order to reestablish your toddler's sense of security, be consistent with discipline. She needs to know that she can count on enforcement of the rules if she disobeys and that you are still the loving and consistent parent you have always been. Verbalize your trust in her ability to meet your expectations, for example, "I know you can remember to clean up your toys when you are finished." Then provide support to ensure success, such as, "Let's work together to put away your toys."

Expect separation anxiety.

When the toddler saw his mother getting ready to leave, he would begin to sob uncontrollably. He would follow her around the kitchen clinging to her legs as she got her keys and purse to go. He put his face in her skirt and cried. He became more hysterical as the inevitable parting came nearer. This happened every time she left, even though sometimes she would be gone for less than an hour, and other times she would be gone all day.

Your toddler is afraid of being left alone, even though he demands independence. Because he lacks a sense of time passing, he is unable to tell when you will return from a night out or a day at work. If he already feels the loss of one parent, this fear is intensified. One parent has already left the house, and your toddler's worst nightmare is that the other parent will abandon him and leave him alone and defenseless.

(126) Why does my toddler get anxious when I leave?

Your toddler expects constant attention because developmentally he is egocentric. He craves your presence to provide security. The loss of one parent upsets routines and creates insecurity. He may be afraid he will be abandoned by the custodial parent. He acts out these behaviors because he is too young to talk about them.

(127) Will my toddler experience separation anxiety when I go away for only a short while?

Separation will be just as intense if you leave for a few minutes as when you leave for the whole day. Your toddler's sense of time is not well-developed, so his fears are the same for either short-term or long-term separation.

(128) What is my toddler thinking when he refuses to leave my sight?

Your toddler is afraid that if he loses sight of you, he will be unable to find you. He does not trust that you will return. Because he is so dependent on you as his caretaker, separation is very frightening for him. He may also be attempting to maintain your attention and control you.

(129) What is my toddler trying to express when she cries at bedtime?

Your toddler may be afraid that you will sneak off in the night while she is sleeping. She may be afraid that you will leave as the absent parent did and she will wake up alone with no one to care for her. She may be reacting out of fear of the dark and the unknown. Crying can also be a simple strategy to postpone bedtime.

(130) Should I discipline or punish my toddler for separation anxiety?

Instead of administering disciplinary action, give patient assurances that you love your toddler and will return. Do not use threats or bribes. Separation anxiety is normal, so help your toddler master these feelings.

(131) How can I help my toddler deal with separation anxiety?

Being interested in the here and now means that once you are gone, your toddler will become interested in his surroundings and cheerfully go about his business. It is hard to tear yourself away from a tearful toddler, but peek back when you are out of sight. It can be a blow to your ego to be forgotten so soon.

Minimize your separations to those that are necessary. Provide as much regularity as possible until your toddler reestablishes a sense of control. Develop rituals for separation. He usually will be distracted once you are out of sight. Your toddler will sense your anxiety if you let his tears drag you back again and again. He will learn to use tears to control you.

(132) What strategy will work best when my toddler has separation anxiety?

Try to remain calm. This is not always easy when you are in a hurry. Give a hug and a kiss, and leave immediately. Always tell your toddler when you are leaving. Never sneak out to avoid her anguish over separation; it will only prove to her that you will disappear. This will make her cling to you even more, not letting you out of her sight. Remember, she needs to reestablish a sense of security.

Establish routines or rituals.

Routines and rituals in the home can help establish a sense of security for your toddler. The predictability of routines helps her with transition periods. Transitional objects such as a favorite toy or blanket are common at this stage and also help to make the change less stressful.

(133) What are some rituals I can share with my toddler?

At bedtime share a favorite story or listen to a tape. Teach mealtime manners such as putting a napkin in the lap. Instill safety rituals such as looking before crossing the street or buckling up in the car. Establish rituals for gaining your toddler's attention, for example, snapping your fingers or counting to a certain number to get his attention before you give directions.

(134) What are some routines I should avoid with my toddler?

The exhausted mother would finally give in at night and allow the toddler to sleep with her since he woke up every two hours for comfort. She tried to put him in his own room, but he would crawl across the floor after pulling himself out of his bed and drag himself crying down the hallway past a steep set of stairs to her room. This was frightening to the mother, so she gave in for two more years. Soon he was used to it, and she didn't even try to put him in his own bed. At age 4, he was still waking up every two hours. When he was 6, he still woke up every two hours. The little boy would sleep in his room only if his mother did too.

Avoid routines such as sleeping with Mom or Dad. Once a routine is established, it is very difficult to change. Do not let guilt trap you into giving in for short-term peace when you will end up paying a long-term price. Your toddler needs to learn to comfort herself. Use a night light and a special transition object such as a blanket or stuffed animal to help her. Let her cry herself back to sleep if necessary. The crying may seem to go on forever, but it will decrease gradually as she learns to comfort herself.

Conclusion

Your toddler is egocentric and lives in the present. She views the world through her own needs. Her greatest need is to establish independence and control over her world. Adjustment problems following parental separation may create a disruption in this emerging independence. She will often experience separation anxiety or regressive behavior under stress. This is normal and should be handled gently. Encourage her to move forward as she feels more secure. Provide constant reassurances of your love.

As your toddler moves toward independence, she will develop receptive and expressive language skills. Take time to read, play games, and talk with her. She can understand language better than she can express it. Due to limited language and motor skills and immature logic, she will experience many frustrations. She may act out if her demands are not met instantly. Ignoring this behavior while acknowledging her feelings provides love and acceptance. Expressing disapproval of specific behaviors should be separated from expressing disapproval of her. Be alert to signs of a building crisis for prevention of temper tantrums. Remove your toddler from temptations and redirect her attention.

Your toddler can be curious and driven to explore her environment. It is essential to provide a physically safe environment for her explorations. Removing your treasures from her reach may limit conflicts. Help the absent parent, grandparents, and others to child-proof their homes.

As a single parent of a toddler, you will often experience stress and frustration. Utilizing stress reduction techniques can really help. When and if you do explode, forgive yourself and apologize to your toddler. Do not try to win her over with bribes; a hug is enough. If the stress continues to build, seek outside help.

Preschoolers

The two little girls sat in the back seat of the car and argued as they headed for the beach after a busy morning at preschool. "My hair is longer than yours," said the blonde, as she tilted her head backwards to make her long hair reach her waist. "Is not," said the redhead, whose hair was at least 6 or 7 inches longer. "You're making it longer by putting your head back." And so it went for 20 minutes on the way to the beach.

When they got out of the car, they began to argue about the names of the crabs that ran from their footsteps—"ghost crabs," "blue crabs," "fiddler crabs," "calico crabs." Each was an authority on the knowledge she had obtained over the vast span of the past 4 years. With a matter-of-fact air, they continued arguing down the beach about mermaids and unicorns until they were out of hearing range, each trying to prove her knowledge of facts about the world to the other.

Two hours later, in the backseat of the car, lying on towels and pillows, exhausted from the sun and ready for a nap, they continued to argue with what energy they had left. "My mommy's a doctor," said the redhead. "Well," said the blonde, resigning herself to exit the conversation and ultimately win completely, "Some day my prince will come, and yours won't!"

The preschool years generally extend from about age 3 to age 5 or 6, depending on developmental differences. Preschool children often have been described as being "in a love affair with the world." They are very active and constantly explore the world around them. They continue to be unable to delineate fact from fantasy and move within both realms as though it were one all-encompassing reality. They become aware of themselves and other people, and their emotional interests begin to shift beyond the family to the world at large.

Preschoolers must relinquish part of their attachment to their mothers and the intense relationship with them that has been the bedrock of their lives. They begin to move from this primary relationship to a more intense relationship with both parents. Their relationships then extend to teachers, surrogate parents, sitters, and other children. They are aware of an expanding community of different people and different roles, new ideas and new problems.

Preschoolers have limited reasoning ability. They are egocentric in their thinking and believe that everything revolves around them—if the sun appears to move, it must move in relationship to them and their demands. They master the developmental milestones of dressing and feeding themselves and also toilet training. Bodily control gets better as preschoolers get older. This is a period of gender-role identification with the parent of the same sex.

Teach decision-making skills.

As your preschooler becomes conscious of his own actions and the consequences of those actions, he also begins to realize that other people have feelings. He begins to understand rules and standards for behavior, and becomes aware of things he should and should not do. For your preschooler, you represent everything that is good and wise in the world. You define what is good or bad, and then he is able to judge when he has made good or bad choices. This skill helps prepare him for the independence and responsibility he will need in grade school.

(135) How can I help my preschooler understand good choices?

Most issues your preschooler deals with are related to her world of family and peers. Teach her that mistakes are wonderful opportunities. Explain cause and effect: "If you do _____, then _____ will happen." Use logical and natural consequences to reinforce making good choices over bad choices.

(136) How does my preschooler understand choices?

Your preschooler defines good and bad by the consequences of the behavior. If it has a good consequence or feels good—for instance, eating a cookie or finger painting with mashed potatoes at dinner time—it is good. If it has a bad consequence or feels bad—for instance, burning a hand on a hot cookie sheet or being scolded for playing with the food—it is bad.

(137) What is a natural consequence for my preschooler?

A natural consequence happens to your preschooler as a direct response to her behavior. For example, if she touches a hot stove, she will burn her fingers. She will learn that the stove will cause pain if she touches it. Behaviors such as this carry natural consequences. Because some of these behaviors are harmful, your preschooler particularly needs protection. She will not learn the lesson through words of caution, no matter how many times she hears them. However, one touch of the stove, and the lesson is learned permanently and effectively through natural consequences.

(138) What is a logical consequence for my preschooler?

A logical consequence is tied to a behavior. For example, you might say to your preschooler: "You didn't pick up your toys, so you cannot have a playmate over because your room is not ready for company." A logical consequence makes sense of reality, such as, "If you don't get dressed to go shopping, you'll have to stay at home with the family or a sitter." Logical consequences are very effective since they are tied to reality and are directly related to the rule broken.

(139) How can I teach my preschooler to understand cause and effect?

Explain real situations and real results, such as: "You did not go to bed at bedtime; therefore, you are tired this morning"; "Because you did not eat your lunch, you have a stomach ache"; "You did not pick up your toys, so I have to do it, which means we do not have time to go out for ice cream." With practice, your preschooler will get better at understanding cause and effect, but remember he may not always match the right cause with the right effect. This is a problem when the cause and effect are separated by time, because he thinks in the here and now. He may also have problems with ownership of his behavior. He may pass blame for a bad choice to someone else. For instance, "The dog (cat, ghost, troll, etc.) ate the cookies."

(140) Is my preschooler too young to solve problems?

Your preschooler solves problems every day. Foster this behavior by praising him when you notice him in the process of solving problems. For example, say: "You and your friend both wanted the red crayon. You decided to take turns. You let your friend use it first. That was a very good way to solve your problem." Talk out loud in the presence of your preschooler as you go through the small steps of solving problems. This will give him insight into breaking down a problem into small bits so that it can be solved. For instance, you might say: "I spilled some milk on the table. I could leave it there, or I could clean it up. I think I will clean it up. I want to use the table when I make cookies. It will be nicer to use the table if it is clean. What do I need to clean the table?"

(141) How can I help my preschooler make wise choices concerning strangers?

Your preschooler does not have a firm understanding of the word "stranger." Once she has introduced herself, she may consider anyone her friend. If she craves attention, she is particularly susceptible to the friendliness of strangers. Your preschooler needs to understand that a stranger does not always look like a monster and may seem friendly. It is a difficult task to balance the need to protect her with the need to prevent excess anxiety about strangers. Remind your preschooler often of the need to avoid strangers. Together watch cartoon videos designed to help explain the concept of strangers. Use cues from the video as discussion starters.

Guide behavior with discipline.

Your preschooler needs models of appropriate behaviors and choices. He also needs guidance and feedback about the choices he makes. Discipline can be used to help him learn to make better choices. Discipline from you is essential to helping him develop self-discipline.

(142) What is the difference between punishing and disciplining my preschooler?

Punishment is designed to be punitive, to hurt, and/or to cause either physical or emotional pain. It is usually inconsistent, a spur-of-the-moment event, with anger or frustration as the driving force behind the action. Punishment is driven from crisis to crisis with no clear consistency or fairness. It can foster resentment in your preschooler and guilt for you.

On the other hand, discipline relies on adult leadership and authority, structures that promote success, and strategic reactions. It establishes family structure with procedures, routines, rules or expectations, and consequences. Discipline is intended to teach values and behaviors and is planned in advance, often in conjunction with your preschooler. It allows you to plan reactions to misbehavior in advance and provides clear and consistent consequences to rule-breaking behavior. Ultimately, discipline is far more effective because your preschooler knows in advance what the rules and consequences are, thus freeing you of the need to choose a punishment every time a misbehavior or crisis occurs. Good discipline is really training for self-control and self-discipline.

(143) What forms of discipline will be effective with my preschooler?

Discipline should be consistent and should teach your preschooler negotiation skills and responsibility. Following are examples of effective disciplinary methods:

- *Give alternatives*—"Do you want to clean up the mess or spend 10 minutes in your room while I clean it up?"
- *Use prevention strategies*—Put a warning sign on the cookie jar: ⊘ or "NO."
- *Incorporate time-out*—"You need some time to calm down and think about this behavior. Please sit in the time-out chair for 5 minutes." Set a timer to signal the end of time-out. Then ask, "Are you ready to return to the activity and follow the rules?"
- *Establish a set of rules and consequences*—Rule: Clean up your toys. Consequence: A toy will be put away for 1 week.
- *Set limits*—"You may choose a snack. It may be a fruit, a vegetable, or cheese and crackers. It may not be a candy bar or cookies."
- *Anticipate problems in advance for problem solving*—"If you use the fingerpaints in your room, they may spill and make a mess."
- *Teach by example*—"I would like to watch TV now, but I can only watch one show. I'll wait till later and watch my favorite show."

(144) What is reparation discipline for my preschooler?

Reparation discipline requires your preschooler to repair the damage she has done. For example, you might say, "You broke the sitter's toy, so you will have to give her one of yours to take its place." Reparation discipline is an effective and fair form of discipline, particularly when your preschooler is involved in establishing the rules for behavior.[1]

(145) How will I know if my preschooler really understands family rules?

Early on, your preschooler will understand when he has not met standards of behavior. As he approaches school-age, he will develop the ability to identify good choices or bad choices. Because he is driven by egocentric needs, however, he will often make choices based on expediency. He will consider the risk of getting caught. Observe your preschooler looking around for witnesses before grabbing candy from the candy rack. Monitor his understanding of the choice and decide what motivated the behavior. Adjust your response to fit the motivation. If he chooses the candy because he thinks he won't get caught, respond with: "Sometimes we get caught doing bad things and are punished right away. Sometimes we are not caught, but we feel bad because we know we did something bad."

(146) What message is my preschooler sending by misbehaving. How can I deal with the misbehavior?

When your preschooler misbehaves, one of four motives is usually behind his actions: He is seeking attention, power, or revenge; or he feels inadequate.[2]

If your preschooler seeks *attention* by interrupting you when you are on the phone or talking to guests, use logical consequences (ex.: "You may stay in your room while guests are here and miss your snack"), allow for natural consequences (ex.: Ignore him and continue to talk), or redirect behavior (ex.: "Would you please go outside and watch for the mailcarrier?").

If your preschooler becomes defiant in searching for *power*, he may refuse to go to bed or to school. Do not get into a power struggle. Instead, present consequences (ex.: "You must go to bed now. You will not get storytime").

If your preschooler perceives he has been treated unfairly, he may seek *revenge*. He may break a sibling's favorite toy or hide your keys. Communicate openly with him. Build trust. Practice feedback. Listen to the feelings behind the words, interpret the words, and tell him what you think he meant. For example, say, "I know you are feeling angry, but it is not acceptable to break a toy."

If your preschooler feels *inadequate*, he may tend to give up. He may feel helpless and as if he doesn't belong. Don't criticize him. Rather, encourage positive attempts. Focus on his assets and skills. Set up opportunities for him to experience success.

(147) When should I begin to hold my preschooler responsible for her own behavior?

The preschooler was so looking forward to Christmas. He had been told that if he were "good," he would get a lot of gifts. Jake wasn't sure what "good" meant, but he had hoped Santa Claus would think he had been good. Sometimes, though, he worried, because the adults around him said he was "bad." He worried like this all Christmas Eve night. These worries disturbed his sleep, and he was fitful in the night as he pondered "good" versus "bad."

The adult members of the family were awake long before Jake. (He had fretted so over his problem that he was up most of the night and was unintentionally sleeping in on Christmas morning due to exhaustion.) When Jake got up and proceeded to the tree with his eyes blinking to focus, he looked around the room in amazement. The question had been answered for him by the amount of presents there. The room was full. It was his biggest Christmas ever! The adults looked on, awaiting his response. He finally said in a daze, "I have been a 'good' boy!"

Your preschooler is able to determine right from wrong and is responsible for her own behavior within limits. Using specific behaviors to tell her what to do (what exactly is expected) is more successful than telling her how to be. Some things she can control, but many things are beyond her control. A chart on the door of her room containing a short set of reasonable rules, complete with picture clues, can serve as a reminder of what to do. For example,

Rules
1. Put toys away
2. Put clothes in basket
3. Close drawers

Consequences for breaking the rules should be just as simple. Emphasis should be on real or logical consequences. Consequences should be tied to the broken rule. If your preschooler does not put her toys away, as a consequence, you will put them away on a high shelf for a reasonable period of time.

Encourage learning through toys and play.

Play is the work of a child. Your preschooler learns from play. It provides the opportunity to try out many roles and also allows him to work out problems. Your preschooler needs a variety of toys, even though his favorite toys may be your tools. He can act out his anxieties by playing with a dollhouse and dolls. Allow him to say whatever he wants when he plays, without adult judgment or criticism. Asking questions such as "Why do you think the doll was angry?" can help you find out the feelings of your preschooler. Watching role play of family members can give strong clues to what he is thinking and can help alleviate your anxieties. Remember, all feelings are acceptable in role playing.

(148) How can I use play to help my preschooler address the emotions that come with the absence of a parent?

Your preschooler will engage in a lot of pretend or make-believe play. This pretend play will give her an opportunity to make sense of her environment. If you observe her playing with dolls or a dollhouse, for example, listen to her verbalization to learn about her feelings. Give important suggestions, such as, "The daddy says he is leaving because he cannot live with the mommy, but he still loves the baby."

(149) What should I do if I notice my preschooler during play showing sad, angry, or confused emotions about the absent parent?

Model or suggest alternative emotions, such as, "What if the mommy doll cuddled the baby?" This may help your preschooler learn new ways to deal with uncomfortable feelings. This kind of playing also provides an opportunity for her to try on different roles. She will often imitate what she sees and hears at home. She will also demonstrate that she wants affection, caring, and concern from the absent parent. Encouraging your preschooler to play the absent parent's role can help her work out her feelings and provide reassurance of love from the absent parent.

(150) What is the role of play in the social development of my preschooler?

Playing helps your preschooler act out his feelings and try new rules. As he moves from the toddler stage into the preschool period, he moves in social stages characterized by the type of play he engages in. Parallel play, or playing alongside another child with no interaction, gives way to associative play. When he is engaged in associative play, he will do things in groups without an integration of activity; for example, his sand play has no relationship to another preschooler's play at building in the sand. They may share space and toys, but they have different goals. Cooperative play occurs when there is true interaction and cooperation. Your preschooler will learn to share, take turns, and work for a common goal.

(151) What is the role of play in the motor skills development of my preschooler?

Your preschooler will develop eye-hand coordination and will become better at playing with balls, bats, rackets, and other toys. The neural pathways to the brain for activities are more efficiently developed at her age than in older children. For example, if your preschooler begins to swing a tennis racket at age 4, she will have a more efficient swing than if she begins to play tennis at the age of 12. "The earlier, the better" is the rule for developing sports and physical talents.

(152) What is the role of play in the cognitive development of my preschooler?

Your preschooler's play is serious business. Play helps to develop cognitive thinking skills through the experiences of cause-effect and problem solving. The saying that "Play is the work of children, and study is the work of students" is evident in the intensity of your preschooler at play. He can become so absorbed in play that he forgets it is a game. The bounds between reality and fantasy do not exist for him.

(153) What is the role of play in the emotional development of my preschooler?

Aggression is a part of your preschooler's play. She may act out aggression in make-believe situations by fighting over possession of toys or changing loyalties and friendships often. She may be well liked or picked on. She may be excluded from one group and included in another.

Through play your preschooler will learn to cooperate and coordinate activities. Leadership qualities will emerge. She may alternate between being a leader or a follower, depending on the group she is in. She will experience conflict. She may become bossy and win the admiration of her peers, while boys her age may try to rule by physical power. She will probably use more words in her conflicts with other girls, whereas preschool boys may show more physical aggression.

(154) What is the role of dramatic play for my preschooler?

Cars were parked near the basketball goal in the long, circular driveway. Several college students were standing around their cars and discussing their courses for the new quarter. The 4-year-old brother of one of the college students quickly recognized the villains in the driveway from the living room window. The mission was clear to him. He donned his cape and mask to hide his identity.

With lightning speed, known only to true superheroes, he ran to the garage to get his tricycle. He headed directly for the villains; no danger would stop him from his mission. He drove straight for the first "villain," the largest of the group. As the other "villains" screamed, the "big one" jumped up on his car just in time to save his shins. The superhero would not stop; he would get them all. He circled back again and again until he had sent each of them up onto their cars, turning the wheels of the tricycle only at the last possible moment. Then without looking back, he left the "villains" in screams of surprise to move on to the next mission of a true superhero.

Because fantasy is so important to his world, dramatic play is a favorite activity of your preschooler He can escape reality, over which he has no control, to the world of fantasy, which he can control, by only thinking it. Wishes play an important part of fantasy and dramatic play.

Your preschooler probably loves costumes and will become a superhero such as Batman or Superman. He will don props that allow him to be a monster or another scary creature. He will become quite animated and will play at being a kitten, a rabbit, a dog, a horse, or a cow. He will delight in dressing in adult clothes and playing the role of a scientist, a veterinarian, a doctor, a mommy, a daddy, a movie star, a good guy, or a bad guy.

Distinguish between fantasy and reality.

Your preschooler gives equal attention to real and make-believe. She does not have the ability to discern one from the other. She may make up stories about the absent parent or imaginary friends or places. This is not the same as a lie. The stories represent childhood reality and provide a way for your preschooler to fulfill her own needs. Storytelling contributes to her sense of security. Simple statements such as "It would be nice if your father could take you on a fishing trip," or "It would really be fun if your mommy took you shopping" can reflect acceptance of your preschooler's thoughts and feelings concerning the absent parent, while gently reminding her that the stories are not real.

(155) Is it normal for my preschooler to tell lies?

> "At school today Superman came into the classroom, and he was on my side," said Jimmy.
>
> The father responded, "Did he help you with cutting and pasting?"
>
> "No, silly, he was on the playground. He couldn't fly into the classroom with the windows closed; he had to come down from the sky," the preschooler patiently explained.

Your preschooler doesn't have the same grasp on fantasy and reality that you have. He may tell "lies" in order to make some sense of the world around him, for instance, "Casper did it; then he flew out the window." There is still some vagueness between what is real and what is unreal for your preschooler, so don't punish him for lying. He might lie in an effort to establish some control over the larger environment. He may say, "The giant broke it and then just disappeared!"

Sometimes a lie reflects wishful thinking. Your preschooler may try to change things through language. Ask questions to help him identify what is true. Ask, "Was it the giant, or was it my big boy?" Make it safe for him to tell the truth. Offer praise for telling the truth, even if you have administered punishment for the confessed act.

(156) What should I do if my preschooler creates an imaginary parent?

Dinner was served. A lady who was a special guest of Daddy's was seated at the table next to Karen. Unexpectedly, the preschooler screamed in fear as her daddy began to seat himself.

"Daddy, you can't sit there. You almost sat on Mommy. Mommy, are you all right? Daddy is sorry. Now what would you like for dinner, Mommy?"

A look of dismay settled onto Daddy's face. It looked as though this dinner might be a bit crowded.

An imaginary parent may simply share some of your preschooler's playtime or may become a major presence in your household. It is not unusual for a preschooler to insist upon a place at the dinner table for the imaginary parent. Accept your preschooler's imaginary parent, but communicate your understanding that this is a pretend or make-believe activity. Say, "It is okay to pretend Daddy can join us for dinner, but not tonight. Maybe we can pretend to invite him for pizza this weekend."

(157) What should I say when my preschooler tells me about things she wants to do with the absent parent?

The mother was driving to the grocery store. The preschoolers were looking forward to an afternoon of play. They planned to play with action figures when they had finished running errands. The two little boys sat in the back of the van comparing fathers. Drew said his father took him to stay with him every weekend, and they always watched movies. Frank said his father always took him to amusement parks. They had been to Disneyland, Disney World, Six Flags, the Atlanta Zoo, the San Diego Zoo, the Bronx Zoo, and so on.

Actually, Frank hadn't been anywhere with his father in more than a year. He certainly had not been to all of those places. He wanted his father to take him, so he wished it and was even able to give details of each trip. His mother remained silent. She knew that he was trying to fit in, and that his fantasies were driven by an effort to boost his image in the eyes of his peers.

Use the strategy of feedback when your preschooler expresses concerns or needs. Repeat the content or feeling she expresses. For instance, say: "You want to have Mommy over for a tea party"; or "You miss your walks with Daddy." This fosters communication skills and keeps your preschooler from bottling up emotions that produce acting-out behavior. Don't just listen; actually hear what she has to say, such as, "When Daddy was little and I was big, I always took him to the toy store." Hearing the message in the words could give you a response such as, "I bet you would like it if your daddy took you to the toy store." If you are wrong, your child will correct you. If you are right, she will feel understood. When she senses that you understand her feelings, she will be able to listen to what you say and will appreciate your efforts.

(158) What should I do if my preschooler has imaginary friends?

It was a morning when the preschooler Candy would not be going to school but would accompany her mother to the pediatrician. Her brother was at kindergarten, and she had complete reign of the house, which delighted her. She requested that she be allowed to cook breakfast, since there was time and there were no interruptions from her big brother. She announced that she had become interested in eating eggs recently and would be cooking eggs for breakfast. Her mother conceded and said that she would be available to assist with the making of breakfast as soon as she had a shower.

Candy was left in the kitchen to play with her little dog, Tiny. Fifteen minutes later, the mother walked into the kitchen showered and dressed. Candy was out of sight, nowhere to be found. In her place was a full dozen eggs lying about in various places in the kitchen. Tiny was also absent.

The mother began walking down the driveway when around the bushes came Candy with Tiny on the leash. The conversation turned to where they had gone and why. It appeared, according to Candy, that Tiny had expressed a need to go out.

In listening to Candy's account of the walk, the mother had forgotten the eggs pelted around the kitchen. As they returned to the house, now too late to either cook or eat breakfast, the mother asked Candy what had happened. "I don't know. It must have been 'Not Me'—you know, Mommy, the little troll who lives in our house." The mother realized that Candy could not discern fact from the fantasy of her teasing about "Not Me," who was blamed for any chaos at Candy's house.

Having imaginary friends is normal for a preschooler. It is okay to acknowledge the "presence" of imaginary friends when your preschooler requests it, but avoid encouraging this behavior. Limitations such as "Your friend may not have a chair at the dinner table" are reasonable. Imaginary friends may be the result of an unmet need, so your preschooler may need more personal attention and also outside friends.

Instill a sense of security.

A little boy sat in a Sunday school class for the first time. He was excited about being able to attend "school" instead of being in the toddler room. He waited at his table expecting good things to happen. He was ready to please the teachers.

A teacher walked in the front of the room and asked the class to draw a picture of their families. The other teachers circled around the room to write labels on figures to identify family members. The children eagerly pointed out "Mommy," "Daddy," "Sister," "Brother." The teacher stopped to help the new little boy. It seemed he had a very large family including "Mommy," "Grandma," "Grandpa," "uncles," and "friends." When she asked where the daddy was, he confidently replied, "I don't have a daddy, but I have lots of other people!" The look on the teacher's face caused the new little preschooler to take his picture away and hide it.

Your preschooler will probably exhibit stronger reactions to the loss of a parent's presence in the home than he would at another age. He is developing initiative and ambition, which will prepare him for success in school and social relationships. He is also developing a sense of guilt and is beginning to understand cause and effect, even though he may not always connect the right cause and effect. His egocentric thoughts may cause him to believe that the parent's absence is his fault. He may revert to behaviors more typical of an infant and/or toddler. He may not only exhibit regression but may develop excessively demanding behaviors as a response to stress. Your consistent love and acceptance are essential at this point.

(159) How should I answer my preschooler's question, "Why is my family different?"

In a matter-of-fact way, tell your preschooler why his family is different and why his parents are not together as in some other families. Respond in a positive way, such as, "Not all parents can be with their children. I'm sure your mother (or father) would like to be with you." Your preschooler will need time and repetition to process this information, so you may have to answer the same question many times. Your accepting attitude during these discussions is important to his ability to understand.

(160) What should I do if my preschooler seems to have loyalty conflicts between me and the absent parent?

Encourage visitation by the absent parent. Support the parent's decisions. Let your preschooler know that you do not expect him to take your side in order to prove he loves you. If you have problems with the absent parent, don't put your preschooler in the middle. Work out problems directly, privately, and away from him.

(161) What should I say to my preschooler who thinks if she is good, the absent parent will return?

Give this explanation: "When two parents decide not to live together, it is an adult decision. This decision is not affected by what children do and cannot be changed by what children do. Since things children do cannot make a parent leave, things children do cannot make a parent return." Give constant reassurance to your preschoolers such as, "You are a wonderful girl, and Mommy/Daddy would love to be here with you, but adults sometimes need to do things you don't understand."

(162) What should I say if my preschooler takes on excessive responsibility around the house after the loss of the other parent?

Children with an absent parent often hear, "You are the man of the house now" or "Your mother/father needs to depend on you now that she/he is alone." This places adult responsibility on the shoulders of a preschooler. If you notice your preschooler taking on adult roles, tell a story such as this:

"Once upon a time, there was a little baby bear. His daddy bear left one day to live in another place. When the daddy bear left, baby bear thought he was the man of the house, but he was really only a little baby bear. He still needed his mommy bear to take care of him, and she did."

Your preschooler may ask to hear the story over and over and may tell you she felt the same way baby bear felt. You can reply, "Isn't that silly?"

(163) How can I give my preschooler a sense of belonging to a family when one parent is absent?

Create networks of support for yourself and your preschooler. The family can be extended to include the larger family (grandparents, cousins, and so on). These members may increase in importance as one parent leaves the home. Also, godmothers and godfathers may take on increased importance as the nuclear family changes. Very special friends can be considered family members as well. Support can come from neighborhood organizations.

One preschooler without a father asked her grandfather to be her daddy so she could fit in when friends talked about their fathers. When she was asked about her daddy, she talked about her grandfather. This sometimes caused confusion for adults, but it made the preschooler feel "just like everyone else."

(164) What can I do to help my preschooler deal with anxiety over the absent parent?

"Mommy, I don't want to go to school. I have a stomach ache. I don't feel good." Lately this excuse had become a regular occurrence. The little boy seemed fine at home and at play, so the mother guessed that something must be wrong at school. She drove to the preschool and spoke with the lead teacher. The mother was honest and told her that Bobby was acting "school phobic."

After brainstorming together for a while, the mother and teacher figured it out—the preschool was heavily preparing for the father's luncheon. There were skits, plays, songs, and a program to welcome the fathers to the classroom. Artwork was being created in honor of the fathers, and a special lunch would be prepared by the class for the fathers to share when they came for the program. Bobby felt left out. He felt as though he didn't count because his father lived far away and couldn't come. The teacher invited her husband to attend as Bobby's substitute father. Bobby's school phobia seemed to disappear when he felt part of the Father's Day luncheon.

Encourage your preschooler to remember and talk about the good times with the absent parent. You might say, "Remember when you and your dad went fishing?" Share pictures or souvenirs of times the family shared before the absent parent left the household. Keep a basket of items such as ticket stubs, popcorn boxes, and receipts from visits with the absent parent for your preschooler to have and enjoy.

(165) What should I do if I have difficulty recalling good memories of the absent parent?

If it is difficult for you to handle your preschooler's need to reminisce, encourage older children in the family to do this. If no older children are present, then perhaps you could provide a scrapbook to help your preschooler feel closer to the absent parent, and your participation may not be needed. Suggest that she get out the scrapbook when she is feeling insecure. Encourage her to draw pictures to send to the absent parent or to contact the absent parent directly.

Enlist other adults to serve as gender role models.

The preschool boy had found some business shirts his father left behind. He managed to button up a shirt, which hung around his ankles. A red paisley tie went around his neck. His own red high-top tennis shoes completed the outfit. He wore a straw hat and an old pair of his father's reading glasses he found in a desk drawer. He carried the Sunday paper under his arm. He looked quite the little man.

He watched for a long time in the mirror in his mother's room, where he could see all of himself, and he was quite pleased. As he studied the image and pretended to read the newspaper, glancing up from time to time to study himself, it occurred to him that his father probably did not wear red high-top tennis shoes. After pondering this problem for a bit, he went to the closet to find some men's shoes—although he wasn't sure what they looked like since he had not seen his father for more than a year.

Frank finally decided to take this problem to his mother. He found her in the study. She was pleased with his attire. He obviously had a problem because his face was puzzled, and he seemed overly concerned with where his father was and when his father would come to see him.

His mother patiently explained that his father was busy and couldn't visit right now. "Then how will I know unless I see him?" asked Frank "What do you need to know, Sweetheart?" asked the mother. "What kind of shoes does my daddy wear?" Even though Frank didn't see his father, he was bonded to him as a role model. He wanted to wear the same shoes as his father, even though he did not know what kind of shoes those were.

The mother, being sensitive to this, showed pictures of the father to Frank. The next time they were in a department store, she showed Frank the shoes his father wore.

Gender-role identification is a developmental need of your preschooler. He needs positive role models to spend time with him and to model activities that are sex roles of the absent parent. This also satisfies his need for male or female adult attention.

Sometimes your preschooler may be drawn to all males/females in search of a parent figure to replace the absent father/mother. He will tag along behind a plumber, a mechanic, or a nurse, trying to satisfy his need for male or female attention. The need for physical contact with both males and females is important for him.

Family group outings provide an opportunity for you to supervise these contacts. After church on Sunday, a nurturing minister can give a few minutes of attention to your preschooler. Church family activities during the week provide another source of contact. Grandparents, aunt and uncles, and older cousins may act as same-gender role models.

(166) What is the role of family in the development of my preschooler?

The role of the family is to provide opportunities for your preschooler to develop skills. He needs a variety of male and female role models and also the freedom to try on new roles and act out feelings through play. Because he is greatly affected by the absence of a parent, he may develop feelings of guilt and responsibility for the breakup of the family. Give constant reassurance of the love of both parents.

(167) How will my preschooler develop gender-role identification?

Your preschooler will begin to understand various gender-role standards from role modeling by males and females. By observing adult role models at this age, he will identify with another person, usually of the same gender, whom he chooses as a model. He will be particularly intense in this identification if he feels he has the same qualities or characteristics of that person.

(168) Is it necessary for my preschooler to have an adult of the same gender in the home in order to identify gender roles?

Your preschooler will not learn all of her gender-role behavior from the same-gender parent. She will also be influenced by the parent who is the most competent of the two parents. She will find admirable qualities to value and emulate in grandparents, aunts, uncles, and neighbors who have a caring relationship with her.

(169) If one parent is absent most of the time with little or no visitation, how can my preschooler establish a role model?

Theoretically, your preschooler does not need the daily presence of the same-gender parent in order to develop appropriate gender-role behavior. She will be exposed to a variety of role models in her daily life and consequently will experiment with many roles through play as she develops a sense of identity.

Guide your preschooler to select several appropriate role models in the extended family and in the church and/or community. Try substituting an uncle, aunt, a grandparent, the parent of another child, a coach, a minister, etc. of the same gender as a "significant other" person with whom she can identify. Participate in family-type activities such as: single parent groups or family dinners at churches, community service events, family picnics or cookouts, and fund-raising events for charitable causes. Mingling with other families gives your preschooler the opportunity to observe same-gender adults and can open the door for many questions and dialogue between the two of you.

(170) Are gender roles imposed on my preschooler by societal expectations?

The toddler could talk, but it was very difficult to understand her. She had shown her single mother that she could be quite willful. It was going to be interesting raising Missy. This particular morning she was in a screeching rage. She was seated on the kitchen counter, and her mother was dressing her. The outfit was made of blue jean material, with pink buttons and a lining of pink-flowered material so that the cuffs of the pants would be pink if they were turned up. A pink t-shirt was under the overalls. She pulled at the overalls and began to sweat in frustration, turning her honey-brown-gold curls dark with perspiration. The sobbing was quickly moving into hysteria.

The single mother felt overwhelmed by her schedule and could clearly see that it would not be kept if this continued. She began to take the edges of the overalls up and look underneath for pins or labels that might be sticking in Missy's arms or legs. She could not find anything, though her probing had somewhat quieted Missy. She guessed all was well, only to have Missy escalate when she tried to stand her on her feet.

Bordering on hysteria, the mother began to undress the little girl. She quieted and was consoled with this turn of events. The overalls were laid aside, and the mother tried another pair of pants and a shirt, "NoNoNo!!!" Missy shook her head emphatically. The mother thought that maybe this was a wardrobe thing.

To test her guess, she went to the closet in Missy's room and returned with two pink dresses. Missy stretched out her arms to the party dress and hugged it to her face as though it were a favorite teddy bear. "What was wrong with these clothes?" asked the mother, more in tune to Missy's explanation. Just then her brother walked in. Missy graciously picked up the overalls and handed them to her brother. "Boys' clothes," said Missy. To her, denim was for boys and did not reflect her idea of being feminine.

Societal expectations may be imposed by the media, grandparents, or caregivers. It is difficult to avoid these influences, although your preschooler will explore a variety of roles and may alternately play with dolls and trucks. Adults in her environment will encourage traditional roles through gifts, words, and actions. Even when you are careful to minimize gender-role differences, gender-role identification takes place. Your preschooler will discover her gender and explore all of the things it means to be that gender. She will notice physical differences during preschool years and will probably ask some questions. Openness on your part during this natural phase will help develop an atmosphere of trust and comfort. She needs the assurance that one's gender does not limit one's choices and opportunities in life.

Conclusion

Your preschooler will begin to explore the world outside his family, even though he still sees the world from his own egocentric perspective and has limited experiences and reasoning skills to guide his exploration. Help him learn to make choices and exercise self-discipline in his explorations. Use natural and logical consequences to help him learn about cause-and-effect relationships. Guide his behavior choices with rules and consequences you determined previously.

Much of your preschooler's learning will come from toys and play. Play helps foster social, motor, cognitive, and emotional development and also provides a way for him to express his feelings about an absent parent. Because play is so important at his age, your preschooler will have difficulty discriminating between fantasy and reality. He may make up stories or imaginary characters. Accept this behavior and gently guide him to understand the difference.

Your preschooler will also learn about gender roles and will incorporate these into play. Even though you may not impose gender-role values on him, he will make his own determination through advertisements, television, magazines, and watching the world. He will decide what it means to be a boy or a girl. His interest or lack of interest in gender roles will be determined by available role models as well as heredity or a natural propensity to do certain things. Providing your preschooler with opportunities to be with same-gender role models is important, particularly if the parent who left the home is of the same gender as your preschooler. Role models can help give the extra attention he needs to meet his security needs. Engage the assistance of the absent parent and other adults.

Notes

[1]Kevin Lehman, *Making Children Mind Without Losing Yours* (New York: Dell Publishers, 1984).

[2]Rudolf Dreikus, *Fundamentals of Adlerian Psychology* (Chicago: Alfred Adler Institute, 1960).

Elementary
School Children

The kindergarten class bustled with activity. The walls were colorful and bright. Several children marched to music.

It was activity center time, and some children were in the housekeeping area with the baby dolls. Being the most intent group in the room, they attracted the teacher's curiosity. She moved closer to them so she could listen to them as they played.

"Let's pretend," said one of the girls to her friend. "I'm the mommy, you're the baby, and there's not a daddy."

The little boy nodded and said, "The daddy went away."

The other little girl said, "I want to be a mommy, too. Let's pretend we are both mommies, and we'll take our babies shopping."

"Yes," said the little boy, "and there's not a daddy."

"Yes," replied the two girls.

"The daddy can be on an airplane," said the little boy.

"Will he come back to this house?" the first little girl asked.

"No, he'll only go back to Ohio, and I won't ever see him again," said the little boy.

"The baby is sad," said the second girl. "She wants her mommy."

At this point, the teacher redirected their attention. "Let's put your baby dolls in the stroller for your shopping trip."

The kindergarteners picked up their baby dolls and went to find the strollers. She heard them discussing what store they would visit. She breathed a sigh and made a note in her planning book to mention this incident at parent conference time. She knew that all three children lived in single-parent homes. She would have to provide some special attention for them during the year.

As children make the transition from the preschool stage to elementary school, they are still functioning at what Piaget[1] referred to as the preoperational stage of development. They continue to be very egocentric and have difficulty distinguishing between fantasy and reality. They use play to act out their fears and to explore new ways of viewing the world.

The transition from preschool environments to more structured elementary school environments at age 5 begins a period of rapid intellectual and social growth for children. Around age 7 they enter Piaget's concrete operations stage of development. They begin to think and solve problems more logically and objectively.

Individual differences may affect adjustment to the demands of elementary school. Some children experience problems in academic or social adjustment. When children begin kindergarten, they must learn to deal with teachers and other adult authority figures at school. Most elementary school teachers are female. Male administrators or principals in the elementary school often serve as disciplinarians rather than nurturing figures. School may call for a difficult adjustment for male students since teachers tend to show more disapproval of boys during the early school years. In our social structure, boys are generally allowed more freedom to show aggression and independence than girls. These behaviors, however, are not acceptable in the elementary classroom.

Children in the early elementary grades need a lot of freedom to move and exercise growing bodies. Schools, however, demand a lot of sitting still. Girls are usually socialized during the preschool years to conform and to seek approval for good behavior, so this makes the adjustment easier for them. Boys find the adjustment more difficult, however.

In addition to academic adjustment, elementary school children will face social adjustment challenges. They want to fit in with their peers. A parent's leaving the home during this time will affect children's peer relationships and may adversely affect schoolwork. Parents will face challenges and must learn to step back gradually and help their children move toward independence and success in school.

Prepare your child
to succeed in school.

The mother was awakened before the alarm went off. Her young daughter was tugging at her shoulder and eagerly repeating, "Come on, Mom. We'll be late for school!" The mother looked up to see her excited 5-year-old dressed in her new "first day of school" clothes. She had already eaten breakfast and put her new backpack on her shoulders. The mother dressed quickly and then walked the child to the school bus stop. She documented this special event with her camera. She was taking one last picture as the bus pulled away and her smiling daughter waved goodbye from the window. She watched until the bus was out of sight. As she turned to walk home, she wiped a tear from her eye.

There is much more to getting your child ready for school than buying new clothes and school supplies. You will have a new role in your child's life. You will need to help her feel productive and experience success to develop a good feeling about herself as a learner and worker. She will need reassurance that she is a "good learner" and will ask for this reassurance constantly. She will look to her teachers as well as her parents for this approval.

(171) How can I help my child make the transition from home to kindergarten?

Provide experiences for your child to learn social skills in an environment such as a day-care center or a play group. A preschooler typically engages in solitary or parallel play. She either plays alone or has learned to share toys and will play next to other children. In kindergarten she will learn more cooperative play activities.

Because moving into a new environment can be very scary for your child, in the spring before kindergarten her preschool or day care program may take a field trip to local schools. Your child will have the opportunity to see the building, meet the teachers, and even try out the cafeteria. Schools also sponsor kindergarten round-ups. These round-up weeks generally focus on the school's need to fill out paperwork and evaluate your child's readiness for school. You can help ease the transition for her by arranging visits before the structured round-up. Also participate in kindergarten orientation during the week before school begins to help ease the transition.

On the first day of school, walk your child to the school bus stop and wave goodbye. Save your tears until she is out of sight. If you drive her to school the first day, explain that you will take her to the classroom and then go home or to work. Do not hang around. If she suspects you are worried, she will worry, too. Schools have trained the staff and made plans to ease the transition for even the most tearful kindergartener. Your child soon will be happily engaged in a new experience.

(172) How can I help my child make the transition from kindergarten to first grade?

Kindergarten is activity-oriented. A kindergartener learns through play and active involvement with learning material, whereas a 1st grader learns through more focused attention on academics in a paper-pencil format. If your child has difficulty sitting still for extended periods of time, this can interfere with his success in school. You can prepare him for success by "playing school" together and taking short (2-3 minute) turns being the teacher and student. Model how you work quietly when you are the student. Praise him when he plays the student and works quietly. Provide simple paper-pencil activities (ex.: matching, tracing) for your child to do during family activities such as church or waiting in the doctor's office. If these are simple enough to ensure successful completion independently, you will be helping to increase his perseverance and attention span.

(173) How can I prepare my child for the world of academics?

Schedule time to read together every night. Reading at bedtime can become a lifetime habit. If you choose the book carefully, reading it will increase your child's knowledge and vocabulary, give you a chance to show her how much fun reading is, give her a chance to unwind, and give you something special to share together. Share picture books and predictable children's stories that capture your child's attention. Let her choose books from the children's section of the library. Ask the children's librarian for suggestions based on your child's interests and age level. Some of the classic novels, although written on an adult level, have become well-loved stories for children. You can read the classics to your child until she can read them alone. *Treasure Island, Alice in Wonderland, Wind in the Willows,* the original Grimms Brothers fairy tales, and others have an appeal to adults as well as to children. You can share a section or chapter each evening.

(174) Do I have to be a reading expert to help my child learn to read?

You do not need special training to help your child learn to read. Include him in family reading time when all family members read silently. Ask him to read to you. This provides an opportunity for him to develop oral reading skills. Take turns reading a page or a chapter. Act out the "parts" of the characters in the story.

Whether you read or your child reads, pause frequently to ask questions such as: "What do you think will happen next?" "Did he mean to break it?" "What would you do if you were the character?" Pause to provide information, for instance: "Tom Sawyer lived before they had TV"; or "A meter is about one yard. Let me show you how long that is." Encourage your child to stop regularly to summarize or paraphrase material in his own words. Make him an active rather than a passive reader.

(175) How can I fit in reading time when my schedule is already overloaded?

Play tapes of favorite stories while you are riding in the car. Have your child read to you while you are doing chores. Don't worry about mistakes; mistakes are part of the learning process. When your child has difficulty with a word, ask him to cover it with a finger and read it again, "The sun is _____," and try to guess what would make sense. This practice will help him use context to learn new words and will give you a chance to provide a word. If this doesn't work, ask him to spell the word aloud. This will teach him to pay attention to the whole word and will help you provide the word without leaving your task.

Ask an older child to read to a younger child. This can provide your older child with extra oral reading practice while keeping the younger sibling entertained. Encourage the younger child to read to an older sibling. Young children often will tell stories about the pictures or recite from memory familiar stories. Have your child call his grandparents and read to them over the phone. Send tapes of the child reading to the absent parent or other relatives.

Save the last few minutes of the day to read to your child. The time will create a love of reading and pave the way toward becoming a successful student.

Support your child's school experience.

Schools tend to attribute all problems a single-parent child exhibits at school to a "broken home." Your home is *not* "broken." Your family is whole and functional. Counteract this myth by becoming involved in your child's education. Involvement may be indirect, such as teaching him the importance and value of an education, or direct, such as teaching him skills for school success.

School is a collaboration between you and your child's teachers. His teachers spend all day with him and can keep you informed about his academic and social development and help you identify problem areas that need to be addressed. When you show interest in your child's education and support the teachers and staff, they will be more likely to give him the extra support he needs, and he will be encouraged to succeed.

(176) How can I help my child succeed in school?

Your elementary school child needs constant feedback. Specific positive feedback is more helpful than general praise, for instance: "You did a nice job of remembering to have your notes for school signed last night. That helps us to be ready for school in the morning without problems." Statements such as these tell your child which specific behaviors are "good" and should be repeated. General praise statements such as "You were good this morning" don't define "good behavior," and they can backfire if she has broken family rules without your knowledge.

Maintain contact with your child's school and teachers. Let them know that your child's success is an important priority with you. Be involved. Attend workshops and other events. Contribute your time or talents to the classroom. For example, send materials related to a certain topic of study, share a favorite book with your child's class, donate a book, volunteer to read a book to the class, or share information about your hobby or career.

Attend parent-teacher conferences. Seek to involve the absent parent. Present a united front. A parent-teacher conference can include both parents and their new spouses in a discussion of ways to help a child with academic problems. If a joint conference is not possible for all parents, have the parent with available time or skills meet with school officials, and then share the information gleaned from the conference.

(177) What can I do to help my child's teachers?

It is difficult for your child to pay attention in class when he is pre-occupied with family problems. Let his teachers be aware of problems at home so that they can be sensitive to him at school. The more teachers understand you and your child, the better able they will be to help your child become successful in the classroom.

(178) How can I get teachers to help my child succeed?

Teachers want to help your child succeed. Meet with them to discuss ways you can work together. Discuss ways to help your child become ready to learn in school. Ask the teachers to complete a daily progress checksheet. They may allow your child to come into their classrooms before school and help them set up for the day. A special time such as this can help your child feel like an integral part of the classroom and can give her the security she needs to fit in.

(179) How can I help my child get along with his teachers?

Some of your child's teachers will be warm, flexible, and nurturing. Others will be less tolerant and no-nonsense. Some teachers will have rules similar to the ones at home. Others may have an entirely different set of rules. Sometimes adjustment to various personality styles of teachers can pose problems for your child.

Teach your child to accept the different styles of teachers. Practice "teacher-pleasing behaviors" with him. Explain that making eye contact when someone is talking is a sign of respect and interest. Role-play paying attention and making eye contact by taking turns being the teacher and student. Your child may find it difficult to wait his turn in a discussion or when he wants help. Teaching him cues for when to talk in class, such as how to avoid interrupting someone who is talking, may help him learn patience. If the teacher insists on hand-raising, practice this at home.

(180) What can I do to help my child through adjustment problems at school?

If your child is having trouble adjusting to school, visit the school. If this is not possible, send a note to her teacher once a week and mention that you are available to help in the evenings with your child's schoolwork. Ask if there are specific areas in which she needs extra help. An early elementary teacher is more likely to involve you in adjustment problem issues by providing more frequent and detailed communication with you concerning observed problems. An upper elementary teacher generally expects a child to solve her own problems. Support your child's teacher's efforts to promote greater independence. Maintain communication with the teacher, but do not expect him to solve the problems for your child.

(181) Does it help to visit my child's class or have lunch with him?

Your child will probably love the opportunity to show off his parents. He will be proud that you came to share in his day. When you pay attention to his classmates, he can gain status in the group. Teachers will be aware of your concern and interest in his progress.

Help your child solve academic and social problems at school.

As your child begins school, she will move into a world of academics full of new ideas and the acquisition of new skills. Sometimes schoolwork will pose problems for her. She will learn skills that are the building blocks for all learning, such as how to study, how to organize assignments, and how to follow through on assignments. She will need to learn to be focused, motivated, and willing to ask for help.

In elementary school your child will also face expanding social demands. She will become increasingly sensitive to "fitting in" with her peers. Learning the social skills for participation in groups is essential to your child's self-concept.

(182) How will I know if my child has a schoolwork problem?

Check your child's backpack or book bag each day for homework assignments and notes from teachers. Many elementary teachers send completed work and/or progress reports on academic and social behavior each week. If your child's teacher has not established this routine for the entire class, request that she do it for your child. Review the progress report and work with your child. Let her show off her favorite activities and discuss the ones she did not like. Watch for incomplete work or low grades on activities. Discuss your concerns with your child's teacher.

If your child complains of vague physical problems each morning and whines about going to school, this could indicate a school problem. She may not have be able to tell you exactly what is bothering her about going to school. Listen carefully to her complaints to understand what is causing the problem.

(183) What kinds of school problems could my elementary school child experience?

Because your child is from a single-parent home, he is more at risk for development of academic and behavioral problems at school. His academic progress may be affected by a lack of concentration at school. Family change may cause him to be distracted by personal concerns, making him unable to focus on schoolwork. Such problems do not occur only during the initial change but may occur later because of other stresses in his life. Behavioral problems may include withdrawal or acting-out behavior. Feelings of guilt and low self-esteem can lead to withdrawn behavior, or he may seek attention at school and be disruptive.

(184) Are school problems always related to being from a single-parent family?

Most problems in school are not caused by being from a single-parent family. Your child may experience academic problems because of the mismatch between his readiness or learning style and what is going on in the classroom. He may need more repetition or more concrete experience before he can master new academic material. Your child may experience behavioral problems because he has difficulty paying attention for long periods of time in a classroom or he likes to be the center of attention. If he is experiencing problems, ask school officials to convene a child-study team to address his needs. A child study team is a group of teachers who meet to discuss ways to help students exhibiting academic or behavior problems. Attend the team meetings when they discuss your child to get ideas on how you and the teacher can support his learning or behavioral needs as a team. If the team identifies academic or emotional problems that require more intensive intervention, request a Section 504 plan for your child. It guarantees your child's right to "reasonable accommodations" within the classroom to help him succeed.[2]

(185) Why does my child need to fit into a group at school?

Fitting into the group is necessary for your child to feel worthwhile. If she doesn't fit in, she will have difficulty practicing the social and emotional skills needed later in life. Feelings of belonging are also essential to development of a positive self-concept. If your child feels left out, she may be distracted from academic pursuits. Cooperative group work activities can help her learn and practice skills for social success. These activities will teach her to take turns, listen, and work with others.

(186) How will I know if my child has problems with group work at school?

Communication with your child's teacher is essential to identifying group work problems at school. Your child's teacher has the opportunity to observe your child each day in a variety of social settings. She can provide information on his ability to get along with others. Ask specific questions such as: "Does my child prefer to work alone or with others?" "Does my child exhibit appropriate skills during group work?" "Do you assign groups, or do the children pick members?" "Do other children seek out my child for group activities?"

Also ask questions of your child, for instance: "Do you prefer to work alone or with others?" "Who do you like to work with?" "What do you like best/least about group work?" Listen for signs that your child feels a sense of belonging to the class group. Remember that at this age he will switch "best friends" frequently and will have good and bad days at school. If your child consistently expresses feelings of being left out, discuss the problem with his teacher.

(187) What should I do if my child reports teasing from her peers because she is from a single-parent home?

Children can be cruel. They may tease a child who can't share stories about "fishing with Dad" or "making cookies with Mom." Fitting in with a peer group is very important, and your child may lie to cover up. The effects of the teasing or lies will be the same: your child will feel pain. Information is the best weapon you can provide. Explain the differences in families to your child, and discuss ways your family is special. The more comfortable she feels about her family, the stronger her self-confidence will be. Teach her to use humor, for instance: "My dad is allergic to fish"; or "My mom and I tried to make cookies together, but they wouldn't fit in the phone."

(188) How can I help my child learn to respond to teasing or bullying from other children?

Teasing may also focus on issues not related to the single-parent family. Elementary school children can be very cruel and pick on other children for no reason. It is very painful for the child who is teased and for you as the parent. Resist the urge to intervene directly at first. Your child needs to learn to handle such problems independently. Discuss with her ways to respond to the teasing. Role play ignoring teasing or avoiding a bully. Encourage her to ignore the teasing if possible since "tattling" usually leads to more teasing. Most children who tease are trying to show their power and are looking for a reaction. When they are ignored, they will move on to another target. If they see your child respond emotionally, they may escalate their attacks. Your child will be resistant to the negative effects of teasing if she has high self-esteem. Remind her that she knows the teasing is not true.

(189) What should I do if my child needs outside help to stop teasing or bullying from other children?

Your child's safety is your first concern. If avoiding the situation or walking away does not solve the problem, you may need to intervene. If teasing occurs on the school bus, ask an older sibling to ride next to your child, or ask that your child be seated near the driver. If the teasing occurs on a walk to school, have your child walk across the street from the other children or make arrangements for him to use a different bus stop. An older child needs to remember that a bully is often a coward. Ignoring him or telling him directly to stop and then walking away may be effective in stopping his behavior. If this doesn't work, discuss the problem with school officials and the parents of the child who is teasing or bullying your child.

(190) How will teasing affect my child's schoolwork?

If your child is left out of the peer group, picked on, or teased for not fitting in, he may experience learning problems. He may have difficulty concentrating on schoolwork. If he is experiencing school problems or feelings of isolation as a result of teasing, it is time for adult intervention. Discuss with his teacher ways to prevent opportunities for teasing. His teacher could change seating or activity grouping arrangements to limit opportunities. Suggest that your child and his teacher set up a private signal (for example, your child scratches his ear when teasing begins) so that the teacher may use proximity control (such as moving near the children) to stop the behavior. The teacher or school counselor may include lessons or share books about the problem of teasing in class. Your child will not be singled out and may be relieved to hear during the discussion that other children in the class express similar concerns about teasing. Intervention at the group level is most effective since it can limit the bully's power in the group. If your child continues to feel isolated, you may want to consider professional counseling to support him through this difficult time.

(191) How should I approach my child about a school problem that seems to be emotional in nature?

Have a series of one-on-one discussions with your child. A trip to the ice cream shop can provide the opportunity for private conversation. Ask specific questions about school. For example, rather than asking, "How was your day?"—which always gets a response of "Fine"—ask, "What did you do for your science experiment in class?"

Sharing an anecdote from your childhood can open the door to discussions. Your child may not have the vocabulary to express his feelings, but he can identify with feelings you share.

You might say: "When I started in 3rd grade, I had a lot of friends, and I loved my school. Then my parents moved to another neighborhood. I didn't know anyone in the neighborhood or in my new class at school. I was sad. I missed my old friends. And I was afraid the new kids wouldn't like me." As a result of hearing about your childhood, your child may express his feelings about a move to a new school when his parents separate.

An anecdote such as the following may open discussion on learning problems your child is experiencing in school: "I always liked reading when I was in school. I was good at reading aloud, and I used to volunteer to read in class. I wasn't as good in math. I hated it when the teacher asked me to go to the board to solve a problem."

(192) Why should I ask questions about school if my child doesn't want to talk about it?

Asking questions gives you information about what is happening in school and can get your child to tell you about any problems he is experiencing. The question "What is wrong with you?" has no answer; it is an accusation. If you really want to talk to your child, ask questions about details of the school day, and soon you will learn everything. Listen closely. Take time to reflect on what you hear to show that you want to understand. Help your child find a solution. Encourage him to identify a way to solve his problem, and then provide support in carrying out the solution.

Develop methods to ensure your child's success at school.

As school demands increase, your child will be less available to do chores around the house. Cut back on your expectations. Homework should be a first priority. Establish a routine for completing it and also for bedtime and getting ready for school. Allow time for physical activities, socialization with other children and with adults, and extracurricular activities. But don't overload your elementary school child with structured activities such as Boy Scouts or Girl Scouts, sports, or lessons. (Single mothers tend to do this in an attempt to help their children with sports or other activities typically shared with fathers.) Help your child maintain a balanced lifestyle, which will in turn help her be successful in school.

(193) How can a morning routine help my child do well in school?

A routine will help the morning go smoothly so that you send your child off calm, happy, prepared, and ready to learn. Give her a good breakfast to "fuel" learning activity at school. Encourage her to have all materials available and in her backpack before going to bed.

(194) How can I get my elementary school child out the door on time so that I can be ready to go to work?

Establish a morning routine that starts the night before. Place book bags, jackets, raincoats, snow boots, umbrellas, and so on beside the door. Have your child decide on breakfast the night before. If he chooses cereal, put it on the table along with a bowl and a spoon. On a bedroom chair place items he will wear the next day. (An older child can be responsible for these duties.)

(195) What kinds of homework routines can help my child succeed in school?

Decide on a consistent time and place for homework. You may want to establish different times and places for each child in the family according to his or her developmental needs. A younger child needs more adult supervision and assistance. She may need to complete her homework in the kitchen while you prepare or clean up after dinner. Her homework time should be early so that she can get to bed at a reasonable time.

An older child may have a homework area set up in her bedroom or in a quiet room in the house. It should contain any materials and resources needed for schoolwork (dictionary, paper, colored pencils, etc.). Homework time should be adjusted according to your child's needs. As homework demands increase, she may need a break before completing it. Try some homework before dinner. Let her have a break for dinner and household chores and then finish her homework while a younger sibling is getting ready for bed. You can then be available for assistance or checking the older child's progress before bedtime.

(196) How can I keep up with my child's schoolwork when I work all the time?

Take time to discuss your child's schoolwork when the two of you are together. Make valuable use of the time you spend in transit, driving or walking to the bus stop. Drill the multiplication tables. Call out spelling words. Use little pieces of time to do two things at once, one of the things being school-related.

(197) What should I do if my elementary school child is having difficulty concentrating on his homework?

Your child spends 6 hours a day concentrating on schoolwork. In addition, he may spend up to 1 hour on a school bus. It is normal for him to have trouble concentrating on homework at night. You can help by trying to make homework more fun. Make a song or rhyme of the lessons. Make a game of spelling words. Practice homework on the sidewalk using chalk. Provide support and a quiet environment for homework time. He may need to get up 30 minutes early to do homework if he loses concentration at night.

(198) What should I do if my elementary school child does not complete homework assignments?

Your child may not complete her homework because of your family schedule, lack of supervision from you, fatigue from helping you run errands after school. Let her teacher know why she did not complete the homework or that she was frustrated because she didn't understand an assignment. Because she probably will face a consequence at school for incomplete homework, communication with her teachers can help them make modifications when these problems occur. Indicate your willingness to help your child make up the homework on the weekend when you have more time.

Sometimes your child may not complete homework because she chooses to watch TV or play during homework time. She may not bring work home or may not admit she has any. Help her solve her problem through natural consequences such as poor grades and teacher-imposed consequences or through logical consequences such as no TV privileges or play time on school days.

(199) How can I help raise my elementary school child's grades?

Let your child know that you think school is important. Try to spend time checking her progress on homework each night. Limit television time. Keep a supply of library books to read. Read aloud to your child, or have her read to you each night while you are doing chores. Help her with new words and concepts in her reading.

Help your child develop
social skills at school.

Your child's school as a whole and her classroom specifically have a climate that can either encourage or discourage development of proper social skills. Without clear limits concerning treating others with respect, a less assertive student will have trouble with bullies. Without rules to guide behavior, unfairness can result, making it difficult for your child to learn or develop friendships. Remember, she will fit into *some* peer group, so guide her into the groups that have the values your family holds in priority.

(200) How will I know if the social climate of my child's school is good or bad?

Teachers, administrators, paraprofessionals, parent volunteers, office staff, and demographics of the student body make up the climate or atmosphere of your child's school. When you walk into the school, you will notice if the halls are bustling or empty, if the walls are brightly colored or stark, if the children seem cheerful and happy or quiet and sullen. You can notice the dynamics between the children with each other and between the children and the teacher. You can tell if there is camaraderie or if the children seem to be alienated.

(201) How can I ensure that my elementary school child is developing positive friendships?

Meet and approve of your child's friends. Insist on meeting their parents before she can spend time in their homes. Observe your child and her friends at play. Look for shared interests. Watch for bossy or bullying behavior. Observe your child after visits with her friends. Does she happily chat about shared activities, or is she withdrawn or angry?

(202) How can I know if my elementary school child is having problems with other children?

Sometimes your child will tell you, "No one likes me at school," or "I don't like P.E. or recess." These are sure clues that she is being excluded by other children. If you suspect this is a problem, ask her to discuss it. Listen carefully. Validate her feelings. Clique groups do exist at school. They exclude certain children, and everyone gets a turn at being excluded, even the most popular children. Help your child react in a way that doesn't allow exclusion to become a habit. Invite the children who are excluding her at school to participate in a special event with you after school, such as going to the park or watching a video. This breaks up the snobbery and gives your child a chance to create friendships on her own turf. Teach her that the best way to get rid of enemies is to make friends of them.

(203) What should I do if my child is excluded from peer groups at school?

If the groups or cliques at school are excluding your child for being from a single-parent home, talk to the counselor and teacher. Tell them how painful it is for your family to have this happen and ask for their support. Sometimes teachers can structure activities that will end this behavior, such as making your child the team leader. Counselors often conduct sessions on topics such as divorce, making friends, or dealing with stress. Usually they can help you work out a solution. Address this concern immediately. If children get into the habit of excluding another, it can become a bigger problem.

(204) What should I do if others tell me my child is a bully?

Because you want to believe the best about your child, your first reaction to negative reports about him will be disbelief. You will feel defensive, since negative reports about him reflect poorly on you. If you lose your cool at this point, you are modeling inappropriate behavior. Respond to negative reports in a neutral fashion that supports your child but does not ignore the one complaining, for example: "My child has not been raised to be a bully. I am sure there is a misunderstanding. I will talk to him about this."

Talk to your child. He may not understand how his behavior is viewed by others. Sometimes his behavior is a reaction to what others are doing: He may be defending himself or trying to fit in with a group. Be alert if the behavior reflects stress or emotional problems. Remember, a bully is looking for power, attention, or revenge.

Support your child's development outside of school.

Involvement in activities outside of school is essential for your child's development. After all, "All work and no play makes Jack a dull boy." It also causes stress when he doesn't have outlets for his boundless energy. Activities such as individual and team sports can provide opportunities for your child to develop motor and social skills. Scouts or special interest clubs can contribute to his cognitive/intellectual development. Church activities will help his social and spiritual development. Some activities may involve the whole family. Others can provide your child with a chance to develop independence. The most important goals should be providing opportunities for him to do something he enjoys and that will enhance his self-esteem.

(205) What is the importance of extracurricular activities for my elementary school child?

Extracurricular activities provide the opportunity for your child to develop friendships, social skills, sportsmanship, leisure skills, team membership, and leadership. They may also provide the opportunity for family time as you cheer in sports events or attend a choir performance. Your family can benefit from being around other families and developing a greater support network. You may benefit from listening to other adults (from single-parent to dual-career families) who share the same parenting concerns.

(206) What activities are best to boost my elementary school child's self-esteem?

Individual sports are excellent. Any sport that doesn't have a "team" connotation can be a good activity for your child. Some individual sports are karate, swimming, track, bicycling, golf, and tennis. Individual sports lend themselves to individual instruction, which can be a real power booster for your child.

(207) Should my elementary school child participate in organized sports?

Organized sports provide the opportunity for development of athletic skills, teamwork, sportsmanship, and friendship. Depending on the personality of your child, however, organized sports may or may not be a good idea. She may be very successful and thrive in organized sports, but if she is not successful, she may feel left out.

Usually, coaches are parents of players. If the coach's son or daughter gets the most attention and the best positions in the games and at practice, your child may experience further feelings of rejection. Some coaches, however, are nurturing individuals who can provide your child with acceptance and attention. They can help boost self-confidence, regardless of athletic skills.

(208) What should I do if I don't have time to be involved in my elementary school child's extracurricular activities?

One problem with extracurricular activities is the demand on your limited resources of time and money. Scheduling transportation to activities and finding time to practice these skills at home can add stress to an already crowded family schedule. This problem is compounded when there is more than one child to schedule.

When there's just not enough time to work extracurricular activities into your family life, encourage activities at home that will help develop motor skills and ball handling skills. Buy a basketball or an all-purpose ball. Ask your child to practice dribbling with you in the driveway. Usually, other children will join in. Before you know it, your driveway will be a ball field or basketball court. Encourage your child to develop motor skills. Praise him for progress in things such as running fast or jumping rope.

Your child will probably be thrilled with the freedom to make up his own rules and play according to his own schedule. Encourage skills such as teamwork and sportsmanship during family or neighborhood activities. Develop family traditions or shared hobbies to encourage development of leisure skills.

Enforce your rules and consequences.

Your journey as a single parent will be easier if you are consistent. This does not mean you are perfect or that you always do the right thing at the right time. It does mean, however, that you have established discipline guidelines for yourself and your child. Remember that discipline does not mean punishment. Discipline is guidance to train your child in self-control. It means establishing clear rules and consequences to guide you when a problem occurs so that you don't let anger rule.

(209) What is meant by being consistent with my elementary school child?

The behavior of your elementary school child is governed by her perception of "right and wrong." She believes very strongly in the importance of rules and consequences and being fair. She expects consistency in application of rules and consequences. She will be more upset by exceptions or arbitrary application of rules than she will by your enforcement of the rules. It is very important that you not establish rules or consequences that you are not willing or able to consistently enforce. Consistency means that you will use clearly defined rules on which you will rely in moments of crisis. It also means using the consequences for the rules on a regular basis. When your child displays unacceptable behaviors, she needs your guidance to understand what is and what is not acceptable.

(210) What is the benefit of a set of rules for my elementary school child?

Rules provide clear guidelines to define what is "good" or "bad" behavior. Your elementary school child wants to be "good." Specific praise for following rules, for example, "You remembered to get all of your school materials ready before you went to bed last night, and now you are ready for the bus early today!" is more helpful than general praise such as, "You were good this morning." Specific praise helps your child know what behavior choices are "good." Remember when your child breaks a rule, however, to reassure him that he is "good" although the behavior he chose to exhibit may be "bad." These guidelines and your feedback when he follows rules prepare your child for self-control.

(211) How will rules help my elementary school child feel secure?

Your child will be comforted by knowing what is expected of him. Rules keep you from relying on impulsive decisions. You have already decided in advance what is important. Your child needs to know where the limits are. Consistent limits provide a feeling of safety and security in his expanding world. He will often test the limits just to be sure they are still there.

This behavior is typical of elementary school students and is very evident in public schools when they have a substitute teacher. They will test the limits to make sure the rules are the same with the substitute. If the substitute does not firmly and consistently enforce the rules, the students will continue to act out until they know how far they can push.

This behavior is also seen at home when you are most tired and stressed out. Your child may test you to reassure himself of your love. Having previously established rules to help you respond during times of stress is helpful for you and your child.

(212) What should I do if my elementary school child breaks the rules?

Immediately and consistently enforce your rules. When your child breaks a rule, remind her of the rule and the consequence for breaking the rule. Explain what rule she broke and why it is important. Remind her of the consequence for breaking the rule. Keep it brief! Her attention span is limited, so she will "tune you out" if you begin to lecture. Remember, your elementary school child believes in rules and consequences. She needs to know that she can count on you to enforce these rules and consequences in a calm manner.

It is important to understand why your child broke the rule. Sometimes she may make an impulsive choice and feel remorse for the behavior. Reassure her of your love, but enforce the consequence with a reminder that this will help her remember to think about consequences before she acts next time. This is part of training your child for self-control. At other times, she may be acting out to get your attention. Model self-control by quickly reminding her of the rule and enforcing the consequence. You don't want her to learn to use inappropriate behavior to get your attention.

(213) What should I do when my elementary school child purposely breaks the rules to bring about a reaction and/or to test my limits?

When your child breaks rules to get your attention, be firm and consistent. Reassure him of your love, but focus on the need to follow rules. Model self-control. Do not raise your voice. Do not threaten or bargain with him. Let him know that he cannot control you. If he refuses to accept the consequences, enforce a time-out. If he won't go to time-out, remove yourself from the situation temporarily. Explain to your child that you need some time-out to calm down. Then go into your room and lock the door. This allows you to cool down, and it provides a model for how to handle stressful events. When you have calmed down, handle the situation according to your rules and consequences.

(214) What can my elementary school child learn from consequences?

Following through with administering consequences will help your child understand cause and effect. You can approach broken rules in an unemotional manner and administer the consequences calmly. If your child is testing you, she will be looking for any signs of doubt. Stand strong, hold your ground, and let the pieces fall where they may.

(215) How will my elementary school child learn right from wrong?

Your elementary school child probably has rigid standards for right and wrong. He is struggling to establish a sense of moral values and cannot deal with shades of gray. He expects consistency from you in enforcing rules. This contributes to his sense of security and teaches him self-control. He will see the consequences of his actions and thus learn to control those actions.

In addition to teaching your child about rules, guide him in understanding right from wrong so that he can make independent decisions. Briefly explain why a behavior choice is right or wrong, for example: "I understand that you found the remote control car by the bus stop. But you know that it belongs to your friend." Then help your child identify a way to make a better choice, for example, ask, "What do you think you should do with the car?" If he cannot come up with an acceptable choice, present some options, for instance: "I know I would feel bad if I lost my car. I would want someone to return it." "I might call and ask my friend if his car was missing. If he had lost his car, I could tell him I might have found it. Then I would return it." Be careful not to moralize or order your child to "do the right thing." It is important to guide him to make decisions that reflect your family value system.

Provide supervision for your child.

Your elementary school child will begin to venture away from home, eager to spend time with her friends away from your watchful eye. It is important to provide her with opportunities to develop independence, but she still needs supervision. Establishing a balance between supervision and control is a difficult task. You need to formulate some clear rules and consequences to guide you and your child. You also need to establish contacts with other parents so that you can be assured of her safety in their homes.

Insist on knowing the whereabouts of your child. A digital watch with an alarm can remind her to check in at regular intervals. A list of phone numbers of her friends can be helpful if you need to check on your child. Allowing your home to be a gathering place where neighborhood children come to play can also help you know where your child is.

(216) How can I know where my elementary school child is during playtime?

Set certain geographic boundaries for your child. Establish rules for playing that can help you monitor her behavior since you don't have time to watch her play. Be conservative; tell her that she is allowed to go a certain distance. Walk the distance with her several times several days in a row. If you live in a neighborhood with a busy street, you may expand her play area by allowing your child to go through the neighbors' yards (with permission). If she is not allowed to go near the busy street, reinforce this boundary daily. Every time she goes out to play, remind her to stay within the boundaries. When you can go with your child, or if another parent is watching, give her special permission to go beyond the boundaries. Boundaries may limit her behavior, but as she gets older and more responsible, she will be used to self-imposed limits that are part of the rules. If you can be effective in this guidance, you will have more cooperation concerning where your child goes as a teenager later.

(217) What should I do if my elementary school child leaves the house without my permission?

If your child leaves the house without telling you or asking you, help him understand that this is a serious offense. He should have a reality check and know that his safety is questionable when you don't know his whereabouts. If he continues to leave home without permission, call the law officers and tell them your child is missing. When he is returned by security or the police, he will understand the magnitude of disappearing without permission. Don't allow him to manipulate you in this way; the stress of looking for a missing child is more than your schedule and demands will bear. One call for help from the professionals may save your child's life by stopping this dangerous behavior, and your sanity may be saved in the process.

(218) What if my elementary school child promises to check in and then forgets?

If you think your child truly forgot, do special things to help her remember such as carrying a watch or an alarm clock with her. If you feel she was testing the limits, let her know that the next time she wants to go out, there will be considerable consequences for not checking in. Give her some reminders from the news about children who were not kept safe. Use this information not to terrify your child, but to build caution and awareness of the dangers that befall not only children but adults.

Manage adjustment problems caused by family change.

Your child will experience adjustment problems. These are normal reactions to increasing independence. She may experience adjustment problems as she enters new social groups and experiences. Particularly difficult is adjustment to change in the family structure. Change causes stress. Stress can lead to changes in behavior. When there is a change in the family structure, all family members must adjust to new roles. Your elementary school child will resist change. Her behavior may reflect her need for stability.

(219) What should I do if my elementary school child gets into trouble?

Your child will learn by trial and error. Sometimes her choices will get her into trouble. You may not know what to do when she runs into trouble. You may feel angry, but you need to control your feelings and focus on the current problem. Your child needs your guidance. Decide what you can do to help or prevent problems from occurring. Keep a cool head.

When your child gets into trouble, you may feel guilty because you have been physically or emotionally unable to meet her needs due to your reactions to the family change. You may have been focusing on your own needs and did not provide the supervision or support she needed. Skip the guilt! This is not the time to dwell on blame or guilt. Rather, focus on the problem and use it as an opportunity to model problem-solving skills.

You may want to protect and defend your child, but protecting her from the consequences of her behavior may only result in repetition of the same wrong choices. If her behavior is an attempt to get your attention, avoid reinforcing this attention-getting behavior. If she gets into trouble, identify logical consequences for her behavior. Assure her of your love, but remain firm in teaching her that such behaviors are not acceptable. After the problem is solved, have a family meeting to discuss ways to avoid future problems.

Involve the absent parent as much as possible during a crisis. Hiding problems from the absent parent will isolate him/her from your child, and such secrets can interfere with your child's ability to develop a relationship with the absent parent. When both parents present a united front, it provides a sense of security for your child.

(220) Will my elementary school child feel different because he is from a single-parent home?

If there are few single-parent children in your child's group, he will have to deal with additional issues in regard to his friends and classmates. If he has a strong sense of identity and feels loved at home, he will have more self-confidence to deal with these issues.

Problems usually develop when the school curriculum emphasizes the traditional nuclear family and does not address other family models. This is especially evident in early elementary grades when the curriculum focuses on family and community. Your child may feel uncomfortable when the school schedules father-child or mother-child events and he has no one to attend. He may feel left out if his reading books present only traditional family models.

(221) What should I do if my elementary school child feels different from the group?

Peer pressure will be a very powerful influence on your child. Any difference she may have from the group can be a source of pain, unless there is clear adult guidance. Provide support for her both at home and school.

Let the teacher know that your child is experiencing problems. Be as specific as possible in describing activities or incidents that make her feel uncomfortable. Recommend books the teacher can share with the class that address single-parent families. Suggest alternate class activities, for example, invite a favorite adult to class activities rather than just a father or mother. Help your child's teacher understand that class projects focusing on family activities or Mother's Day or Father's Day may cause discomfort for some children.

Provide support at home as well. Discuss issues of concern with your child. Sharing a book about single-parent families may be a good ice-breaker for such a discussion. Reassure your child that it is okay to have a different family structure. Talk about the unique and special things about your family. Help your child feel good about herself and her family.

(222) How will my elementary school child adjust to family change?

Although your child is gradually becoming less self-centered in her view of the world, she will still find it difficult to adjust to change. She may feel responsible for the breakup of the family. She may exhibit signs of stress such as sleeping or eating problems, illness, or lack of energy or interest in activities. She may display immature or acting-out behavior. Since she is still not able to verbalize her feelings, her behavior is a clue that something is bothering her. You need to look beyond the symptoms to address the cause of the stress.

Minimize changes in your child's daily routine. Don't change meal and bedtime routines. It is tempting to set up trays and eat in front of the TV to avoid the missing place at the table. It is also tempting to let your child sleep with you to ease the pain. These changes only create more stress. Stick with your previous routines. Look for ways to strengthen these routines such as setting a more festive table or including your child in food preparation and clean-up time as a shared family activity. Use a tape of the absent parent reading a story to replace the shared story time before the family structure changed.

(223) How will change in family structure affect my elementary school child's relationship with the absent parent?

Your child may express anger and resentment to changes in family structure. These reactions may be directed toward the absent parent. Your child may express bad feelings about the absent parent. It is important that you help her separate her feelings about the absent parent from her feelings about the change in family structure. Don't let your anger or unresolved feelings contribute to a problem between your child and her other parent. Remind her that the absent parent still loves her, but sometimes adults have to make hard choices. The absent parent did not leave the child, even though s/he left the home. S/he is still the child's parent. Encourage your child to initiate contact with the absent parent by writing, drawing a picture, or calling the absent parent.

(224) What should I do if my elementary school child refuses to have contact with the absent parent?

Your child may refuse to see or talk to the absent parent. She may destroy items given to her by the absent parent or pictures of the absent parent. This behavior reflects anger. Accept your child's feelings of anger, but help her develop more appropriate ways to express her emotions.

If possible, discuss this problem with the absent parent. Your child's rejection will be painful for the absent parent. You want to foster a good relationship between your child and the absent parent to avoid further appearances of rejection by the absent parent. Reassure the absent parent that your child's behavior is a reaction to change. Encourage the absent parent to reassure your child that she is loved by both parents, even if they do not live in the same house.

(225) Will my elementary school child blame me for the loss of the other parent?

At times your elementary school child may blame you for the other parent's absence. He may verbalize these feelings and direct his anger through acts of revenge. This behavior may also be covert. He may refuse to cooperate, but will not verbalize his bad feelings or directly show the cause. These covert behaviors are more difficult to manage because you may not be aware of their cause.

(226) What should I do if my elementary school child uses guilt as a means of manipulation?

If your child tries to manipulate you by using guilt, she may be motivated by her need for attention, power, or revenge. She may play you against the other parent in an attempt to get toys or privileges as proof of your love. Help your child verbalize her feelings so that you can help her find ways to manage those feelings and change the behaviors.

Do not give in to feelings of guilt. Do not try to buy back her love. This only makes her feel more insecure. What she really needs is reassurance that she is loved. This reassurance is stronger when you give it freely rather than as an attempt to win her love.

(227) What should I do if my elementary school child claims to hate me?

Respecting your child means treating her as you would treat a valuable client at work or an adult friend. When you show respect for your child, you can demand that the respect be mutual. This does not mean that she is not allowed to express her feelings.

When she is in enough pain to say, "I hate you," she needs to calm down. Don't overreact. Allow her time to rethink the remark. She may not be angry at you, but you may be the only person with whom she feels comfortable expressing her anger. Teach her more acceptable ways of letting you know that she is having a hard time. You may wish to make a house rule that prohibits her from voicing hate for anyone, along with appropriate consequences for breaking the rule. Remember, anger is a powerful emotion and can be very frightening for your child to experience. Practice "I" messages in response to her anger, for instance, "I feel hurt when someone yells at me."

(228) What should I do if my elementary school child feels anger toward the absent parent?

Be empathetic. Listen to your child. Validate his feelings of anger. Discuss ways to diffuse the anger. Discuss ways to talk about these feelings with the absent parent. Have your child write (or draw) these feelings in a letter, and then set the letter aside for awhile until he is calm and can decide if he is ready to rip it up as a way of letting go of the anger. Be careful to avoid sharing his feelings.

(229) What should I say if my elementary school child voices a desire to live with the absent parent?

If your elementary school child threatens to live with the absent parent, his threat is usually the result of anger. He may mistakenly think you are keeping him from having a relationship with the absent parent. Tell him that you want him to be happy and will not stand in the way of his living with the absent parent. Reassure him of your love and your desire to keep him with you. When he has calmed down, he probably will announce a decision to stay with you.

(230) What should I do if my elementary school child has not heard from or seen the absent parent in a long time?

Unfortunately, more than 25% of the single-parent children in the United States do not have regular contact with the absent parent. Sulking and sadness are sure clues to the fact that your child is hurting. Be strong for her; she needs your reassurance that you have a strong united family whether there are one or two parents. Answer her questions. Emphasize what a wonderful person she is and how the absent parent is missing out on the opportunity to be with a great child. Explain that the absence is not your choice, that you would share her with the other parent. Tell her that even though you wish things were different, you feel richer for having her all the time.

(231) What should I say if my elementary school child brings up feelings of abandonment that occurred years ago by the absent parent?

Listen and let your child know that you understand. Validate her feelings. Empathize. Use reflective listening; repeat the things she says to you. If you validate these feelings by listening, she will sense your understanding. Encourage your child to create solutions about the feelings, and then help her choose the best solution.

(232) What are some ways I can initiate contact with the absent parent?

Send copies of report cards to the absent parent. Share school pictures or pictures of important events in your child's life. If you do not know how to reach the absent parent, send materials to the grandparents, or put them in a special box to be saved for the absent parent.

(233) What is the advantage of contacting an absent parent who doesn't visit my child?

A little mail can go a long way toward helping the absent parent see the value of your child. It may help to introduce the parent to your child's life, no matter how uninvolved the parent is. The real benefit is to your child, who will be relieved to have communicated what is important to her with the absent parent. The rest is up to the absent parent.

Respect your child's need to be accepted.

Peer group acceptance becomes increasingly important throughout elementary school. The same-gender peer group exhibits a powerful force. Competition and group dynamics will play a big part in whether or not your child is happy in school. He wants to fit in with the group. Even though he is learning to separate fantasy from reality, when other children talk about their parents, he may make up stories about the absent parent so that he can fit in with his friends.

Do not challenge these stories in front of your child's peers, but rather discuss the stories in a calm manner later. Save discussions about making up stories for a more private time. Your child needs to learn to resist peer pressure to fit in the group, but you don't want to embarrass him in front of his peers.

(234) What should I do if my elementary school child tells fantastic stories that are obvious lies?

Sometimes your child may make up fantastic stories. His stories may be no more than tall tales. His stories may resemble cartoons or hero shows. This is a harmless use of creativity. Talk to your child to see if he understands the difference between fact and fantasy. If you get a response such as, "I like to make up stories like Daniel Boone did," or "Don't you remember that happened in the Schwarzenegger movie?" rest assured that you may have a budding writer on your hands.

(235) What should I say if my elementary school child asks me to back up an unbelievable story in front of his friends?

The first time your child asks you to back up a story, comply so that she can save face, but suggest in private that she leave you out of those tall tales. Sometimes this is an effort to fit in, and the stories will center around the absent parent. Your child may claim to have gone here or there with the absent parent. She probably realizes the story is untrue, but she feels the need to combat the rejection of that parent in front of increasingly important peers. Discuss other ways to handle situations without telling stories. It may be helpful to seek outside help from a counselor or psychologist to help address this problem.

(236) What can I do for my elementary school child if he is upset over changing cliques and friendships at school?

Groups at school will change. At some point everyone will feel left out. Encourage your child to participate in the groups but to avoid situations in which children are cruel to the child who is the outcast of the moment. Talk about what it feels like to be left out. Give an example of a child who may be an outcast at school but is a friend at soccer or ballet. Teach your child to treat everyone with respect. Model this behavior by not participating in neighborhood gossip.

(237) How can peer pressure affect my elementary school child differently from children of a two-parent home?

Peer pressure becomes an increasingly powerful force in your child's life as she progresses through the elementary school years. She will become increasingly aware of differences that affect status in her peer group. Even as early as kindergarten, she may want to have the "in" toy or game. As she gets older, she may begin to demand certain brands of clothes. Elementary school children can be very cruel when someone doesn't conform to group standards. They will pick on a child who is different. The definition of different may change from day to day. A certain type of notebook or backpack may be very cool one day, but the object of teasing at another time.

Financial and time pressures can make it difficult for you to meet the demands for all of the new fads your child may expect. When you are on a limited budget, you can't justify buying a brand name notebook or shirt that costs 4 or 5 times more than an identical one without the brand name. Also, rushing from store to store to track down the latest fad item takes much time. Stores seem to run out of these items very quickly! It can be very stressful when you finally arrive home with a much desired item, only to find out that it has now lost its status. It is also difficult to weigh the importance of obtaining these status items when you are trying to teach your child a value system that is not based on what you have.

(238) How can I prepare my elementary school child to stand up to peer pressure?

How your child fits in and how others see him will have a powerful impact on how he sees himself. He also needs to feel secure enough to resist negative peer pressure. If he has a strong sense of identity and self-concept, he will be able to discriminate when peer pressure is negative. He will respond to peer pressure in a way that creates a comfortable situation within the social structure.

Prepare your child to stand up to peer pressure by reinforcing the importance of who he is, not what he has. Emphasize his positive attributes. Help him identify important attributes in friends. These guiding principles will be very important in preparing him to make choices when peer groups begin to pressure him. Help him understand that peer groups may shift and pick on a different person the next day. Share a book about peer pressure and rejection with your child. Talk about the characters and how they handled the problem. Discuss ways you handled the problem when you were your child's age.

Help your child find alternate ways of expressing anger.

Because of the absence of one parent, your child may feel a lot of anger and resentment toward both parents and perhaps toward life in general. She needs to know that it is normal to have these feelings, but they have to be expressed in a safe and socially acceptable way, such as through exercising, pounding a pillow, writing the feelings down, drawing pictures, or using toys.

(239) What should I do if I find it painful to have discussions with my elementary school child about his emotional outbursts?

It is often difficult for you as a parent to discuss emotional outbursts when you don't feel in control of your emotions yourself. You may need to look for help in controlling your emotions so that you can be a better role model. Consult books for expert ideas. Participate in a support group that can help you identify ways to deal with your feelings.

If you make your child feel that his emotions are forbidden or wrong, he may deny or bottle up his feelings, which can lead to physical illness or accident-prone or explosive behavior. Teach him that there is no one "right" way to control his emotions, that they are a very important part of who he is. Identify constructive ways to express emotions. Model proper ways to deal with emotions: Count to 10. Give yourself time out to cool down. Take a walk. Write a letter to express your feelings, and then put it aside until a later time when you are calmer. Teach your child to accept his emotions, but also to find outlets that won't harm his health (repressing the emotions may only lead to headaches) or his relationships (yelling at others may damage relationships).

(240) What should I do if my elementary school child is withdrawn and won't talk about her anger, but explodes with her playmates?

When your child's anger begins to interfere with her social and emotional development, you need to provide immediate support. Try to observe her or ask her teachers or other adults to report on exactly what takes place when she explodes. These observations may provide clues to what the behavior means. Do certain play activities, for example, playing house, set off the explosions? Do comments from her playmates upset your child, for instance, "You can't be the daddy because you don't have a daddy"? Look for behavior clues.

A pattern may not be evident. Since your child still lacks the ability to express her feelings in words, try playing a game with her and verbalizing what you are doing. Have the toys act out situations. Let your child use a toy to respond. Puppets may be helpful here. Books may also be helpful vehicles for discussions. It is easier for you and your child to discuss the characters rather than yourselves. If your child does not open up in these situations, seek professional help.

(241) How can reading books help my elementary school child learn to express his feelings?

Your child may not have the language skills necessary to describe his feelings. He may not be able to verbalize the reasons behind his feelings. He may feel afraid of his feelings or may fear rejection if he tells someone about these feelings. Reading books about imaginary or real characters who experience these emotions will help your child verbalize his feelings. It will also make him feel comfortable with feelings when he realizes that others experience them, too.

Reading books aloud with your child can open discussion and help the healing process. Discuss the ways the characters managed their feelings. Share your experiences with these feelings. Suggest alternate ways for handling emotions.

(242) What should I do if the books we read don't seem to help my child deal with her feelings?

Enlist professional help from a school counselor, minister, or child psychologist to help your child work through these feelings.

(243) Where can I locate books that discuss issues about the absent parent?

Check with librarians, school counselors, and bookstore clerks for ideas. Be careful when you obtain books about absent parents. Some books on divorce or absent parents may not match your situation. If visitation is the topic of the book and visitation is not a reality for your child, she may become more depressed by reading about it. Books that address single parenting without discussing divorce may be best. The entire population of children cannot benefit from reading one book, but there are a variety of books available to choose from. (See Suggested Readings.)

Give your time and attention, but avoid the "Super Parent" role.

Being a single parent can be overwhelming. You must fill multiple roles. You often feel pulled in several directions. A job is needed to provide financial security for the family. The demands of a job, however, can lead to feelings of guilt when you have to miss out on sharing school activities with your child. Family crises requiring you to miss a day at work, such as the illness of a child, can also cause feelings of guilt. Some jobs require long hours, which complicate child-care arrangements. You may feel frustrated when you have to bring work home. The conflict between the need to attend to work or family is quite stressful. These problems are more intense without a spouse to help with responsibilities. In spite of these competing demands, the greatest gift you can give your child is your time and attention. He needs you more than he needs things.

(244) How can I give more attention to my elementary school child without overextending myself?

Special times reserved for family are needed. Posting this time on a family calendar gives your child a visual reminder. Family mealtime also provides an excellent time for listening to your child. This is a good time to find out about what he is doing in school or after school. Asking questions about his interests and plans and sharing some personal experiences are effective. Turn on the answering machine to avoid disruption during this family time

Family time can focus on fun, such as playing a board game together or taking a trip to the zoo or park. This is an opportunity to set aside time for family meetings to discuss how to spend family fun time. Family time can also focus on everyday activities, such as preparing meals or grocery shopping, or on discussing mutual concerns.

In addition to the reserved family time, take advantage of frequent opportunities during the day for sharing time together. An early riser can enjoy some quiet time with you before the rest of the family awakens.

(245) How can I open the lines of communication with my elementary school child?

Schedule one-on-one time with your child to share a mutually enjoyable activity. Get on her physical level. Sit on the floor and help her assemble puzzles or make clay figures. She will begin to feel comfortable talking to you. Therapists use this method of play as a way to get information from children. Your child will probably tell you things through playing with dolls or mechanical toys that she is unable to express in normal conversation. Puppet play is also very effective, since the role of a puppet is to talk.

(246) How can I enhance communication with my elementary school child?

Listen when your child wants to talk. Treat him like you would a valued friend. Establish eye contact. Give him your undivided attention while he is trying to communicate. Let the phone ring or ask other children not to disturb you for a while. Make comments that show your interest, for example, "What did you do next?" Answer his questions openly and honestly as he starts to develop a more mature understanding of relationships. Your model of good communication skills will help him learn to use them, too.

(247) How can I spend time with my elementary school child when I am not the custodial parent and live far away?

Long-distance parenting requires extra effort at keeping the lines of communication open with your child. Keeping consistent communication is as simple as a phone call. If you call your child every day for 2 minutes, you will have better communication than if you talk for 1 hour once a month, once a year, or sporadically. Some effective absent parents call at the beginning of the day. The early morning is a good time to find your child at home, and it sets the stage for the whole day. If a problem arises during the day, and your child has already spoken to you, she may think of asking you for a solution. If she knows she can depend on your phone calls, she will think of you as a daily parent and as someone who provides support. Also send cards and inexpensive gifts (ex.: erasers, pencil case, a book) in the mail at regular intervals to stay involved in your child's life.

(248) How can I make it up to my elementary school child when I have to work long hours?

You don't need to "make up" time with your child when you have to work long hours or even extra jobs. Focus on sharing time positively. Make the time you spend really count. Give your child your full attention, love, and guidance. Use the time as an opportunity to talk and truly communicate.

(249) How can I be a good parent to my elementary school child when I have so many other responsibilities?

Focus on maintaining a home, not a house. A house can take a lot of neglect and still remain standing. A house is only a physical structure. A home, though, is composed of people who need to feel loved. Focusing on your child, however, doesn't mean you need to live in a pig pen. Teach him to assist with household chores so that the family can spend more time together. Organize the family as a team to clean up the kitchen after dinner, and then use the extra time you've saved for sharing a book or a favorite TV show. Have an older child take over kitchen duties after dinner while you get a younger child ready for bed. Spend the extra time sharing an activity or helping the older child with homework. Teach your child that dividing a large task into small parts helps to conquer it.

(250) How can I juggle my elementary school child's need for activity with my other responsibilities?

In your effort to provide your child with a variety of experiences, you may overschedule him and sacrifice family time. Give your child the freedom to explore a variety of activities and relationships, while allowing for family time. Limit your commitments for structured activities to one per child per season. Your child needs your presence more than your taxi-driving skills. Your child needs some down time, too. Rushing him from activity to activity puts a strain on the whole family, often resulting in the loss of family meals—a great opportunity for communication and sharing—in favor of eating fast food on the road.

Instill a sense of family responsibility.

A single-parent family is like any other family. It is only as strong as its individual members. It is also dependent on shared goals for its success. Your child needs to have responsibility to the family explained and modeled to her. She needs to know the reality of money and time constraints. Reality says there is a time frame in which everything must be done. Reality also says that all bills and expenses must be covered by a certain budget.

(251) How can I teach my elementary school child to take responsibility in the family?

Family meetings can allow everyone to make decisions about allocating family resources and responsibilities. Some of the responsibilities will be allocated to everyone, such as keeping one's room clean. Then, children may select chores they prefer to do, such as clearing the table or feeding the pets. Remaining chores may be assigned on a rotating basis or allocated according to age and skills. For example, older children may do laundry while younger ones help fold. Children need to know that parents cannot complete all of the chores and need help in order to devote more time to the children.

(252) Should I give rewards to my elementary school child in exchange for jobs she does around the house?

If your child contributes to household chores, an allowance can help teach him about the work force and earning a salary. Another reward can be television privileges or activities funded by family resources, which your child earns by fulfilling responsibilities. Develop a list of chores not included in the list of regular responsibilities, such as cleaning the garage, for which extra rewards may be earned. Explain that if you have to pay someone to mow the grass, there isn't money in the budget to go to the movies. If everyone pitches in to mow the grass, weed, plant flowers, and edge the yard, the money you didn't have to pay someone else is money the family can use for entertainment as a reward for hard work. Emphasize development of responsibility and the importance of working together as a family. These values will set the stage for productivity in the work force as your child moves into the future.

(253) *Should I pay my elementary school child for doing chores?*

Your child should not be paid for doing her share of family responsibilities. If she puts successful effort into doing a job that would require a plumber, a painter, or a mechanic, then pay her. That way, she will have the money (or a small part of the money) you would have given to someone else. Now she can buy a new CD or save for a new pair of athletic shoes. You benefit, the family benefits, and your child benefits from a lesson in reality.

Conclusion

Elementary school provides opportunities for your child to develop new skills and increased independence and to explore a broader world. Prepare her for these new experiences by spending time with her at home and reading to her, and then support her school experience by maintaining close contact with her teachers.

If she develops a problem at school, work with her teachers to determine if it is a reaction to family change, a learning or behavior problem that needs to be addressed by a child study team, or a social problem caused by teasing or a lack of social skills. Take time to listen to your child to identify the source of the problem from her perspective.

When the demands of school increase, you may have to cut back on expectations at home and other commitments. Establish morning routines and homework routines to provide support for your child's academic success. Monitor her friendships and problems with other children to ensure her social success. Balance extra-curricular activities with the demands on the family.

Understand that your elementary school child is governed by her perception of "right and wrong," but also that peer group acceptance is very important to her. Respect this need for acceptance, allowing room for increased independence and decision making, but provide supervision at the same time. Continue enforcement of family rules and consequences. Your child depends on you to set and enforce limits on her behavior.

As she expands her circle of contacts, your child may need extra help from you in dealing with social acceptance issues regarding her status as a single-parent child. Help her understand the value of her family structure, even if it is different from her peers'. Involve the absent parent as much as possible. If the absent parent is not available, continue to reassure your child of that parent's love.

Keep the lines of communication open with your elementary school child. Be an active listener and supporter. Help her develop strategies for dealing with her feelings. Spend much time with her, but avoid the "Super Parent" role. Insist on responsibility to her family and shared goals for its success.

Notes

[1]Jean Piaget and Barbara Inhelder, *The Psychology of the Child* (New York: Basic Books, 1969).

[2]Susan B. Brown, *Parental Legal Rights and Responsibilities* (unpublished document, 1997).

Adolescents

Zack was "top dog" at his high school. He was an honors student and a valuable athlete. He was the captain of the football team and excelled in other sports as well. He was highly successful living with a single working mother and seeing little of his father.

In spite of Zack's school success, the constant chiding by boys in the neighborhood and the cruelty of their taunting when his father did not visit during his childhood stayed in his mind. As an adolescent, he was intolerant of other students, but found a positive way to rise above them academically and physically.

His father, who had missed large blocks of time in Zack's childhood, was present at all football games where Zack was the hero. But by then, Zack had no time for his father. It was his father's turn to be left out.

Adolescence marks the transition from childhood to adulthood. During early childhood, children want to grow up to be just like their parents. Therefore, parents need to be very involved in their children's lives. The close bond developed during these years can provide much emotional satisfaction for single parents, but the constant demands on their time and space may become overwhelming, causing many parents to look forward to their children's growing independence.

As children mature, they begin to identify more with their same-gender peers and to assert their budding independence. Adolescents are very concerned with how they are viewed by others and will try to conform to fit in with their peer group. They gradually begin to rebel against parental control. The earliest signs of rebellion against parental control are often conflicts with parents over clothes and chores. These conflicts can be especially hard on single parents who may become caught up in a constant cycle of power struggles with their adolescents.

Single parents don't have another adult in the home to help them deal with the stress. Sometimes a quick phone call to a friend can help avert a conflict with adolescent children. Some problems may sound silly when shared with a friend, but a quick laugh can relieve the stress before the situation gets out of hand. Calling a friend to ask, "Am I crazy to expect my teenagers to maintain a path through the mess in their rooms for emergency escapes?" can help stressed parents see humor in the situation.

Developing a network of other parents, both single and married, can be helpful. Other parents can offer examples of ways they have dealt with similar problems and can help reduce feelings of guilt. There are many hotlines for parents under stress who are without their own support network. Calling one of these hotlines is not a sign of weakness; it is an effective coping strategy to prevent problems.

Understand adolescent development and challenges.

Probably the most difficult task you will face as the parent of an adolescent is managing his constant roller-coaster temperament. He will move rapidly from one emotional extreme to the next, appearing to be controlled by hormonal shifts. This can be a trying time for the family, as he constantly swings from mature to immature behaviors, making it difficult to predict what will happen next.

A typical example may be when your adolescent arrives home from school. He will demand your complete attention as he tells you every detail of his day. Then, as you try to show your interest and ask a few questions, he will attack you for cross-examining him. Just as you adjust to one mood, his behavior will change, and your responses will fuel another conflict. It sometimes seems that you can't do anything right!

It is also typical for your adolescent to expect that he has earned all the rights and privileges of an adult, although he finds it difficult to understand that there are accompanying responsibilities. For example, he may feel that it is his right and privilege to stay out late without calling to check in with you, but if you turn the tables and leave him waiting and worrying, your adolescent will lecture you.

(254) When will adolescence begin for my child?

Signs of adolescence seem to begin earlier with each generation. Your child may exhibit signs of puberty and emerging adolescence in elementary school. The average age is between 9 and 14. The rapid growth spurts and endless appetites are obvious physical signs, whereas mood swings are definite emotional signs. Girls usually show signs of physical and emotional adolescent development at an earlier age than boys. Early adolescence (ages 10–15) is marked by greater extremes in behavior than later adolescence (ages 16–20).

(255) How will my adolescent's school support this developmental stage?

Physical and hormonal changes are occurring at a rapid pace in your adolescent. These changes dominate all systems. She seems to have little energy available for things considered essential by the adults in her life, such as schoolwork. Her middle school program is designed to support children during the early adolescent period. The curriculum and management structures nourish cognitive and emotional development. These programs group students from 6th–8th grades (ages 11–13). Your adolescent is removed from younger elementary and older senior high school students so that her unique needs may be addressed. Middle school curriculum and instructional programs foster the development of multiple intelligence and problem-solving and life skills. They also incorporate cooperative learning strategies and multi-age grouping.

(256) What are multiple intelligences? How can I address this issue at home with my adolescent?

Programs for the development of multiple intelligences promote the idea that there are many ways to learn and demonstrate mastery of a concept. Students are able to experience greater success as they explore concepts through a variety of senses such as vision, hearing, or touch. Middle school educators realize that the psychological and physiological demands on early adolescents may interfere with learning.

Instructional strategies are designed to actively involve students in learning. For example, instead of solving traditional algebra problems, middle schools may involve students in hands-on algebra with a real-life problem-solving emphasis. You can attend school-sponsored workshops about this new approach and then reinforce the concepts by involving your adolescent in real-life problem solving using algebraic concepts at home. An example of a problem might be calculating the number of square feet in your yard to determine how much fertilizer to use.

Parent: How many square feet are in our yard if it is 120 feet wide and 240 feet long?

Child: I don't know how to figure that out.

Parent: Well, let's draw a picture of the yard and then write the measurements. Now we can solve it as an area problem: Area = Length x Width.

Child: Oh, I remember that from school.

Parent: Let's figure that out on the calculator.

Child: The area = 120 x 240. That's 28,800 square feet.

Parent: Great, now let's check the chart to see how much fertilizer we need.

(257) What is cooperative learning? How can I use it at home with my adolescent?

Cooperative learning at school involves a group of two or more working together to solve problems. Some cooperative learning involves a "divide and conquer" model in which each student takes responsibility for part of a large project. This approach demonstrates to adolescents that "the whole is greater than its parts," that others are depending on them to do their part.

At home, your adolescent is involved in cooperative learning when he assists family members in a task, such as preparing and serving a meal and cleaning up after it. He can also be part of a cooperative learning group at a family meeting, for instance, to discuss a sibling or financial problem. The emphasis in these problem-solving sessions is that there is no one right answer, and the group must select one option all members can accept. If all members do not accept the solution, they do not have ownership of the solution. Without ownership of the solution, members will not implement it, and it is doomed to failure. Learning to discuss issues without negative comments is a valuable life skill. Cooperative learning activities at school involve rules on how to communicate and involve all members in a positive way. These same rules are essential to the success of family meetings.

(258) What is multi-age grouping? What does it mean for my adolescent?

Multi-age grouping includes grouping middle school students in teams that cross grade levels and age groups instead of segregating them by grade. Your adolescent may stay with the same students and teachers throughout the middle school years. This practice provides the benefit of a consistent network of friends and teachers for three years and helps your adolescent avoid the stress of trying to adjust to a new group of friends and teachers each year. Teachers have the opportunity to get to know her well and provide more support for her throughout middle school. This strength can become a problem, however, if there are personality conflicts within the group. If problems develop, work with teachers and counselors to identify a solution.

(259) How can I help my adolescent develop problem-solving skills?

Pointing out instances in everyday life that require math skills can help motivate your adolescent. Model the use of math skills. Involve him in selecting the best bargains as you shop for groceries. Teach him to look beyond the "SALE" signs and glitzy advertising to find the best buys. Use the price-per-ounce signs, and then focus on taste or convenience issues as part of the buying decision.

As your adolescent matures, give him a budget for school clothes or other major purchases. Allow him to make personal choices. If you have modeled decision-making skills, he should be ready to make choices with minimal guidance and support. For example,

Child: I've found a great deal. This really cool shirt is on sale.
Parent: You have enough money to buy that shirt. Did you check the care tag? Is it machine washable, or will you have to hand wash or dry clean it?
Child: It says dry clean only.
Parent: How often do you think it will have to be cleaned, and how much will it cost each time?
Child: I guess it isn't such a good deal after all. Let's look for one that is machine washable.

Involving your adolescent in the problem-solving process will prepare him to make good decisions on his own. It will also decrease power struggles over what he considers arbitrary parental decisions. Suppose the parent in the previous example had responded, "No, it will cost too much over the course of time." There would have been no opportunity for discussion—only arguments. Such parental responses usually elicit a pouty or argumentative comeback such as, "You're unfair!"

(260) When should I intervene in my adolescent's problem solving?

Involving your adolescent in the problem-solving process also means that sometimes you have to let him make mistakes. He will learn much more from his own mistakes than from your lectures. He may respond to your questions about the cost of care with an unrealistic response such as: "I'll be very careful, and I can wear it a lot before it needs to be dry cleaned, and I'll pay for the cleaning from my allowance." Past experience will probably tell you that the shirt will end up on the floor after the first wearing and that your adolescent will never have any money left from his allowance to pay for a dry cleaning bill. He needs to learn this for himself, however.

Give your adolescent full responsibility unless danger is involved. A small investment now may pay greater benefits later, and he may actually fulfill his promise and show responsibility this time.

Help your adolescent develop life skills.

Life skills include problem-solving skills and social skills that will help prepare your adolescent to be successful in the outside world. Train her to organize her time, space, materials, and money. School programs often support parental effort since this is an area of great need for early adolescents.

Organization of time is a major area of need. If your early adolescent is typical, she is a master at dawdling away time. She knows the art of procrastination and is very skilled at placing the blame for her failure to meet commitments on everyone but herself. She can spend hours on the phone and in front of videos, computers, and electronic games. You constantly hear: "I didn't have time to do it"; "I've got plenty of time left"; "I didn't know it was so late"; "It was too hard, no one could do it that fast."

Because you live in a time-pressured environment, when your adolescent dawdles and wastes time, you feel the pressures build and conflicts develop. Such conflicts inevitably result in even more lost time. The key to survival begins with understanding that the problem is not your adolescent's rebellion, but a different perception of time.

(261) How can I help my adolescent develop time management skills?

The first step to teaching your adolescent organization of time is your model of a time management system. Distribute calendars to all family members. Meet together weekly to plan schedules. Post a family calendar and daily schedule in a prominent place. Establish a daily checklist of chores to be completed and checked off before free time is given. Block out "no TV, video game, or phone" periods such as before and after school. Allow family members to block out their favorite shows or video game times on the schedule.

After modeling a time management system, encourage family members to develop their own system and follow it. Your input and help are important, but emphasize individual responsibility. Praise your adolescent for effective use of his time. Use specific comments such as, "You had extra time for your friend's phone call tonight because you completed your homework before dinner." Don't worry about offering rewards or consequences for following the schedules—natural consequences will provide a much stronger incentive. Avoid statements such as, "I told you so." Rather, provide specific reminders such as, "You didn't finish your homework because you played video games during homework time." Work with your adolescent's school to develop time management skills. For instance, ask teachers to provide a homework sheet for you to sign each evening.

(262) How can I help my adolescent develop organizational skills?

Organization of space is also a timesaver. Time spent looking for things is wasted time. Teach your adolescent to organize her space and materials by modeling this skill yourself. Invest time and money in setting up storage systems so as to save time and money later. Stock up on notebook paper, dividers, pocket folders, and other school supplies at the beginning of the school year. Help your adolescent organize notebooks for each class. Set up a homework area in a distraction-free space. Store the extra supplies there. Include study aids such as dictionaries or calculators.

Organization of closets, dresser drawers, and laundry areas also saves time. Start with your own closet and drawers to model how an organization system works. Then involve your adolescent in organizing his space. Invest in good hangers so that clothes don't end up on the closet floor each time he rushes through to choose something to wear. Purchase hangers especially designed to hold certain garments or accessories. Consider a specialized storage system for a certain organization problem. Don't expect your adolescent to keep his closets organized all of the time, but set aside time each week to get things back where they belong. Having a place for everything makes this an easier job.

(263) How can I teach my adolescent to organize his chores?

Involve your adolescent in doing his own laundry as much as possible. Provide multiple baskets for sorting laundry. Remind him that he is responsible for taking his laundry to the laundry area. Having to dig through a pile of dirty clothes in his room to find something to wear is a natural consequence for forgetting this rule. Post guidelines for sorting and washing laundry. Provide a basket that holds one load so your adolescent can check the size of a load before putting it in the washer.

Organization of materials can be problematic when there is limited storage space. Ideally, it is more efficient to provide storage near the point of use, such as laundry detergents near the washer and dryer. This efficiency often requires duplication of materials, for example, storage of vacuum cleaners for upstairs and downstairs areas, which can be expensive. Provide a "catch all" basket in strategic places in the house, for instance, at the top and bottom of stairs, to collect miscellaneous items that need to be put away. The key is to identify a storage area that works, and then enforce penalties for failure to return items to their storage area. Fine your adolescent—and yourself—for failure to put things back where they belong. Your model of accepting the consequences for your behavior is a more powerful learning experience for your adolescent than your lectures.

(264) How can I help my adolescent understand our limited family budget?

Money management is a difficult, but essential, skill to model since single parents often struggle on limited resources. You must have the final say in the family budget. Your money management role model is very important. Verbalize your rationale for spending or not spending money. For example, you can say, "I'm tired and would really love to order pizza tonight, but since we want to save money for a movie this weekend, I'll just make macaroni." Stock up on low-cost meals such as spaghetti, and teach your adolescent to prepare these. This will provide help for you and the opportunity for your adolescent to participate in a money-saving activity.

At family meetings, set spending priorities. First, set aside money for essentials (food and bills). Your adolescent doesn't need to know how much money you have or the amount of each bill, just the amount you have available for family discussion. Allow her a voice in how to spend this family money. On a sheet of paper list all suggestions, including a few of your own. After recording all ideas, discuss which ones can wait or which ones are too expensive. Remember, you have the final say, but the more you involve your adolescent in the decision-making process, the more cooperation you will receive.

(265) How can I help my adolescent develop money management skills?

Provide your adolescent with some money of her own. Some families prefer to link the allowance with chores, but it is better to avoid this practice since it leads to arguments over money rather than teaching a lesson in money management. Set the allowance to provide money for charitable donations and a savings account. Teach your adolescent how to fill out savings and deposit slips and to balance her account. Consider using a money management computer program to help plan and implement budgets.

At first, allowance money may seem to "burn a hole in her pockets," and your adolescent may quickly spend it on sweet treats or toys. She may need a limited amount to "splurge" until she has demonstrated maturity in handling money. The natural consequence of poor choices is no money available later in the week for something she wants. Avoid bailing out your adolescent, or you will set yourself up for constant battles over money in the future. She needs to learn the consequences of her decisions.

As your adolescent demonstrates her ability to manage money, increase her allowance and expenses she is responsible for covering. She will need money for social activities with friends or money to support hobbies and interests. At times you may need to provide her with an extra budget amount, such as for buying birthday party gifts or school clothes. Encourage your adolescent to work for extra money or projects. Doing chores for neighbors can be good experiences. She will learn the value of money when she has to work to earn it.

Understand the challenges of late adolescence.

Late adolescence marks a leveling off period in the roller-coaster ride. By late adolescence, physical changes have slowed down. Emotional development is marked by a greater emphasis on relationships with members of the opposite sex, personal communication (i.e., excessive phone use), and grooming habits.

Late adolescence also involves decisions about driving and post-secondary education. Your adolescent will have greater independence in high school but will have to make decisions about what courses to take. He may elect to leave school for part of the school day for on-the-job experience or joint enrollment with a local college. This freedom can put greater demands on the family. Decisions about providing a car and the limitations on use of the car can create stress. Financial issues such as paying for the car, insurance, and upkeep stretch limited resources. Decisions about jobs during the school year must take into account your adolescent's academic and social needs. Increased academic demands and greater involvement in school activities can add additional stress, leaving less time for rest, meals, and family activities.

(266) What educational decisions does my adolescent need to make?

Your adolescent will have to commit to a course of study before he enters 9th grade. Decisions made now impact life decisions later. The decision to follow a college preparatory or vocational track will be difficult to change. Each track requires additional choices such as which vocational option to choose or what level of courses to take in a college preparatory program. Decisions about specific courses within a program are also important. Your adolescent will need to take more math and science courses and courses in technology. A wrong decision can affect his graduation date or which college will accept him.

(267) How can I guide my adolescent to make appropriate educational choices?

Communicate with school counselors to find ways to support your adolescent in making educational decisions. Link her with mentors in the field she hopes to pursue. Many schools provide mentor programs and "shadow days" where your adolescent may spend a day on the job with her mentor. The best assistance you can give during this period is a listening ear and the assurance that you will be there when needed.

(268) How can I cover the financial demands of my adolescent?

The financial demands of your adolescent may seem endless. Many of the demands come from external sources. From lunch money and school supplies to money for yearbooks and sports supplies, the list goes on and on. These demands may stretch your family budget, but they are essentials. Other demands, however, are more internal. Your adolescent has a strong desire to fit in with his peer group. He will insist on having the "right name" brands and labels, or he will be teased. The difference in cost between the "right name" brands and the same item without the "right name" can break your family budget.

(269) How can I involve my adolescent in financial planning?

One of the major challenges in covering the financial demands of your adolescent is teaching him to tell the difference between needs and wants. Needs are items necessary for physical and educational survival. For example, having a sweatshirt in cool weather is a need. Wants are items desirable but not essential to survival. For instance, having a sweatshirt with the right logo is a want. When your adolescent begins his emotional pleas for things he *must* have, it is time for a frank discussion. Have him write a triple-spaced list of all the things he MUST have and then cut the list into individual pieces. Instruct him to divide another piece of paper into two columns and label one as NEED and the other as WANT. Explain the difference between a need and a want. Ask him to place each piece from the MUST list in either the NEED or WANT column.

Initially, your adolescent will place everything in the NEED column. Have him explain the rationale for each need. You may then decide whether you agree, or you may move it to the WANT column. Always take the time to explain your decision if you want this exercise to have value for your adolescent. Because he probably has a very unrealistic idea about the cost of things, it may help if you put a budgeted amount at the top of the page and a price estimate by each item in the NEED column. This will also help him see part of the rationale behind your decisions.

(270) Should I refuse to consider items that are "wants" and not "needs" of my adolescent?

Whenever possible, allow your adolescent to select one or two items from the WANT list to include on your final shopping list. The social pressures to fit in at this age are very important. Compromising on a "right name" jacket or pair of shoes when you can afford it will go a long way toward strengthening her feelings of empowerment within the family. Encourage her to contribute to family responsibilities and the family budget to pay for WANTS. Work out a compromise in which she will pay part of the cost and you will pay the rest. Insist on having her earn the money *before* you purchase the item.

(271) How can my adolescent earn the money for items he wants?

An allowance is a good source of spending money for your adolescent. Have him set aside money for savings, charity, and any expenses for which he is responsible. Allow him to use the discretionary money any way he wishes as long as it is not dangerous (examples: buying skateboards without protective gear) or illegal (examples: drugs, alcohol, or tobacco products). When your adolescent has items on his WANT list that he cannot fit into his budget, offer an opportunity to earn extra money for helping with projects around the house such as cleaning out the attic or garage. Before he begins work on the project, establish in writing an hourly pay rate or fee as well as standards for completion.

Encourage your adolescent to ask for odd jobs in the neighborhood such as babysitting, yardwork, and walking dogs. Establish some ground rules about who he can approach, what kinds of jobs he may accept, and use of your equipment. Remind him of safety rules for use of any equipment and that he may not go into someone's home unless you know the person and give approval.

(272) Should my adolescent have a part-time job?

One of the common WANTS leading an adolescent into a part-time job is the desire to have a car of her own. A part-time job can help your adolescent develop valuable life skills. She will learn about job applications, withholding forms, taxes, and social security. The demands for punctuality, respect for supervisors, and good work habits will expose her to real-life issues. Some job opportunities, though limited in availability, may provide on-the-job experience to test vocational interests for later career choices. Jobs with fast food restaurants and grocery stores, however, are usually easy to find because the rate of turnover is high.

A typical adolescent will work at a job of the latter kind only until she has saved enough money for a special purchase or until she gets frustrated with the job demands. As a result, she does not develop mature work habits. Also, the long hours can interfere with other demands on her time such as homework, family and peer and school activities, and civic and church work.

Have an honest discussion with your adolescent about time and money issues. Emphasize the priorities of health, family, and education. Insist on her getting needed rest, eating regular meals rather than junk food, and exercising regularly. Require contribution to family chores and time for communication and activities with the family.

Prepare your adolescent
for driving privileges.

The freedom of having his own wheels instead of depending on you for transportation to school and social activities is a powerful want for your adolescent. You, too, will feel the freedom when he can provide his own transportation, help transport siblings to and from activities, and run errands.

(273) How can I help my adolescent develop driving skills?

Teaching your adolescent to drive can result in conflict between the two of you. During the learner permit stage, enroll him in a driver education program and/or enlist the assistance of a responsible adult. Establish graduated driving privileges to allow him to demonstrate his maturity and driving skills.

You will face a lot of pressure from your adolescent when he is legally old enough to take the driver's test. He will want to rush right out to get his license on his birthday. Be sure he is ready for the responsibility of driving a vehicle independently. You may want to delay the formal driving test or establish a written contract with him. This written contract should include guidelines for the use of family vehicles and any other vehicles, since family insurance coverage is involved.

Knowing that your adolescent is driving around without you can be a source of constant anxiety. No matter how well he drives when you are with him, the effects of other drivers or peer pressure will contribute to your anxiety. Link driving privileges to demonstrated maturity.

(274) How should I handle the issue of driving privileges with my adolescent?

Restricting driving privileges initially to transportation to and from school and/or a job will allow your adolescent to develop driving experience on familiar routes. Restricting passengers is also a good idea. The distraction of peers in the car may interfere with the concentration required by an inexperienced driver. Peer pressure can also be difficult to manage. Insist on the use of seat belts for all passengers. Set a limit of one passenger at a time. Gradually increase the limit as your adolescent demonstrates responsible driving behavior. Adjust the number as it pertains to transporting siblings.

The hours when your adolescent is on the road is another crucial issue. Traffic and night driving present challenges. Restrictions on types of roads (local to expressway) used may require careful planning of routes. Accompany your adolescent to a new area before he has to drive it alone. Check out any special problem areas. Provide guidance about alternate routes and safety tips.

(275) How should I handle the issue of my adolescent riding with her friends?

Riding with other young drivers may put your adolescent at risk. Some parents decide to let their adolescents drive because they feel more comfortable with their driving skills than those of their friends. Communication with the parents of other young drivers will help ease these concerns. When parents band together to enforce similar rules, their adolescents can't complain that "everyone else's parents let them do it."

Suggest to other parents that they enter into a written contract with their adolescents that covers drinking and driving issues. Seek outside resources that illustrate the danger of drinking and driving. Schools regularly provide educational programs, especially before proms, that illustrate the consequences.

Tell your adolescent that she is not allowed to drink, and that she should not be the "designated driver" for peers who drink. Discuss the importance of taking the keys from friends who do drink and/or contacting a responsible adult to provide transportation. Establish a "no-fault" policy for these situations. If your adolescent knows that she can trust you to help her out in a difficult situation without an embarrassing scene, she will feel secure in calling you. Discuss the problem and the consequence the next day when you both have had time to calm down and reflect on the situation. You must abide by this promise even if she has broken your rules and has been drinking. This is a tall order for you, but it is important to establish trust so she isn't afraid to ask for help when she needs it.

Understand your role in your adolescent's social life.

Karen had been on the phone with her friends for hours. She finally emerged and asked her mother to drive her to the mall. Mother was thrilled. They had so little time together. They were soon on their way. When they arrived at the mall, Karen said, "Just drop me off by the food court." Her mother turned to her in shock, "But I thought we were going to have a chance to look for that sweater you've been wanting." "Mother, please, I can't be seen in the mall with my mother. People will think I'm weird or something."

Your adolescent often will appear to be embarrassed to be seen with you. He will skip family outings in favor of time with his peers. If forced to go out in public with you, he will usually refuse to walk with you. If you provide transportation, your adolescent will sit in the back with his friends and keep his voice low to maintain privacy. He may hang out in groups and prefer public places such as malls or video arcades.

When your adolescent was younger, you knew all of his friends and were directly involved in arranging his social activities. As he matures, he may resent any effort on your part to be involved in his social life. It becomes impossible to meet all of his friends at school or work. Although you should not try to control your adolescent's social life, you should establish some ground rules. Insist on knowing where he is, who he is with, when he will return, any change in schedule or destination, and how to contact him.

(276) How can I get to know my adolescent's friends?

Keep your pantry stocked with beverages and snack foods, and they will come! If possible, provide a place where your adolescent can entertain her friends in relative privacy. Let them be aware of your presence without being intrusive. If your adolescent has trouble standing up for the house rules, intervene and explain the rule calmly. For example, say: "We don't allow smoking in our house. If you feel the need to smoke, I prefer that you go outside"; or "We don't allow that kind of language in our home. I prefer that you not use such language while you are in our home." If the violation continues, ask the rule-breaker to leave. Say, "We don't allow smoking in our house. I am going to have to ask you to leave now"; or "I find that language offensive, and I think it would be best for you to leave now." Remember, it's your home. Your children's friends should feel welcome, but they should respect your home and family members.

(277) What should be my role when my adolescent begins to date?

As your adolescent matures, he will begin to "pair off." When boyfriend-girlfriend relationships develop, couples spend every available minute together. At this point, you need to establish ground rules that protect your adolescent from the temptations of too much time without supervision. Discuss the consequences of too much time alone and ways to avoid them such as keeping busy or having other people around. Inform the other parents of your rules. Provide a place where the young couple can study or spend time together in your home, preferably not a bedroom. Insist that doors to the room remain open.

Choose your battles carefully.

Conflicts between you and your adolescent can end up in shouting matches. At other times your adolescent may withdraw and refuse to communicate at all. A lose-lose situation results. You can sacrifice your relationship with your adolescent when you dominate in the conflict and he is perceived as the loser. Your adolescent also sacrifices the benefits of a relationship with you when he dominates in a conflict and you are perceived as the loser. So choose your battles carefully. Some issues aren't worth the fight. Try to avoid major conflict by keeping the lines of communication open.

(278) How can I communicate with my adolescent?

Most of us are guilty of nonlistening behaviors such as continuing with other tasks while our adolescent is talking. These behaviors communicate a lack of interest in what she has to say. The key to communication with your adolescent is the use of active listening strategies such as listening without commenting and maintaining eye contact to show interest.

Avoid barriers to communication. For instance, phrases such as "I told you so" will cause your adolescent to become defensive. Avoid being judgmental. Don't label him, his behavior, or his friends. These behaviors also bring out defensive responses. Once your adolescent becomes defensive, he will either withdraw or counterattack.

Avoid asking too many questions—an adolescent doesn't like being cross-examined. Leading questions can be threatening, for instance, "Did your friend try smoking too?" Avoid short-answer questions such as, "How was your day?" Show interest by making comments that indicate you heard what he said, for example, "I can just picture how silly that looked!" Encourage your adolescent to talk to you by asking open-ended questions such as, "What did you think about that event?"

(279) What battles can I avoid with my adolescent?

Fights over your adolescent's wardrobe often can be avoided. Involve her in choosing her clothes only after planning and discussing budget issues. Give up some control of style issues, but draw the line at clothes that are too provocative or that violate school rules. Try to remember how you felt at her age. Each generation always follows clothing fads that shock their elders. Following the latest fad is part of the "rite of independence."

Money is always a controversial area. Give your adolescent an allowance to help her develop money management skills. Provide opportunities for her to make extra income, thereby granting some control over her own money. Require that she set aside money for savings and charitable contributions, but allow her complete control over the other funds. When money issues develop, remind her that she has her own money to invest. Many items will quickly lose their appeal when her money is involved.

(280) How can I avoid battles with my adolescent over doing chores?

You and your adolescent probably have very different views about household chores. She may whine about how busy (tired, late, etc.) she is and/or dawdle and procrastinate until you break down and threaten her or complete the chore(s) yourself. Some chores, such as doing the dinner dishes, have to be done in a timely manner. Preestablished consequences, such as loss of telephone time, can be used when you have to complete the chore. Other chores, such as doing laundry, can be left until natural consequences occur such as having no clean clothes to wear.

(281) How should I deal with my adolescent's offensive language?

Your adolescent is constantly bombarded with questionable language from her friends and the media. At this age, she probably enjoys the "shock value" of some words. She may also challenge you to tell her why the language is offensive. Try to approach this issue when both you and your adolescent are calm. Explain reasons for controlling her language, such as for success in school and on the job.

Minimize conflicts over language by establishing guidelines such as, "If certain 'words' make someone uncomfortable, it would be respectful not to use them in their presence." Request that your adolescent refrain from using certain words in your presence or in the presence of other adults at home, church, and school. Establish penalties for violating these guidelines, and enforce them in a fun way during family time. For example, require all family members to pay a dime for every offensive word used, and then donate the collection to a charity. Finally, to save your adolescent's self-esteem and position, try not to correct her language in front of her peers.

(282) What issues require compromise with my adolescent?

Your adolescent's "on-the-run" lifestyle and her need to fit in affect her diet. Diet can become a constant source of debate. This is an area that requires compromise because it involves her health.

Discuss health and diet issues with your adolescent. Provide a healthy diet for your family. Schedule regular family meals as often as possible. Keep lots of healthy foods and snacks on hand. Consider breakfast bars as an alternative to skipping breakfast. Small cans or plastic bottles of juice may be as tempting as soft drinks. Buy healthy snacks in bulk, and package them in individual zip-lock bags for eating on the go. Purchase easy microwaveable meals and snacks such as pizza.

Your adolescent may seem to be a bottomless pit. Her growth spurts may result in apparent overweight one day and concerns about underweight when she shoots up 3 inches overnight! Monitor your adolescent's diet as much as possible, especially if she has special health problems, such as diabetes or allergies, or if you suspect excessive weight loss. Many young girls develop anorexia (not eating enough food to survive) or bulimia (purging food after binge eating). These conditions are very dangerous, and medical and psychological intervention is imperative.

(283) What should I do if I don't approve of some of my adolescent's friends?

Your adolescent's choice of friends can cause many battles. Compromise is needed. You may not approve of all her friends, but refrain from making comments about them. The more you object, the more attractive the friends become. Try to keep your opinions to yourself. However, if you identify friends who are definitely negative influences, you may need to intervene.

Start by calmly discussing your concerns with your adolescent. Try to focus on values rather than personality. For example, say: "I feel concerned when you are out with Jerry and Sue because they drink. I trust that you can make good choices and not be tempted to drink, but you could be put in a dangerous situation if they are drunk." Then trust your adolescent to make good choices. The objective is to set up a situation where she can make the right choice. Provide her with information that may lead her to choose not to associate with these friends. Refusing permission for her to hang out with certain friends is a last resort and is very difficult to enforce.

(284) How should I handle my adolescent's failure to meet curfew?

Your adolescent will expect his curfew to match that of his friends. How late should he stay out? Discuss alternatives with him and then establish firm curfew rules. Establish consequences for failure to meet curfew. Curfew times may be different for each child in the family because of differences in maturity. Set up different times for school nights and weekends. Negotiate a different curfew for special events. Require your adolescent to call home if an unexpected event will cause him to be late. If he fails to meet curfew, it may be a good idea to wait until the next day when you are calmer to discuss the situation. Logical consequences, such as an earlier curfew for a period of time, may prove effective.

(285) What battles are essential for my adolescent's safety?

Smoking is a health hazard. It is also illegal for a minor to buy tobacco products. Remain firm in refusing to finance this habit or tolerate it in your home. Be alert to clues that your adolescent is smoking behind your back. She may do something dangerous such as hide ashtrays under her bed. If you do her laundry, you will notice the smell of smoke and perhaps small burns in her clothes. Confront her about this evidence. She may deny it and blame it on friends. Firmly discuss your objections and rules. Establish and enforce consequences for breaking the rule. If your adolescent has already developed some level of addiction to tobacco, which will make stopping the habit difficult, ask your family doctor to recommend products that can help reduce the symptoms of tobacco withdrawal. If you smoke, consider your model. Demonstrate your commitment by giving up the habit. Enlist your family's help. Set aside the money you would have spent on smoking and use it to buy a special treat for yourself.

Drinking is another health issue. Buying and using alcohol is illegal for minors. This is another area where your model is important. If your adolescent sees you drink, she will ask why it is wrong for her. Emphasize the legal issues, that when she is an adult she can make decisions about alcohol for herself. Until then, she must abide by your rules. Discuss responsible use of alcohol. Emphasize that you don't drink to "get high" or "forget your troubles." Explain the effects of too much alcohol on your reflexes and body. Talk about the dangers of drinking and driving. This is a good time to remove alcohol from your home. The availability of alcohol may provide temptation to try it, especially when there is peer pressure. If you suspect your adolescent is drinking, contact your local Alcoholics Anonymous chapter, which has materials that will help you understand and address this problem. It also has support groups for family members and different age groups.

Drug use is an everpresent danger for adolescents. The same rules discussed for smoking and drinking apply here. Tell your adolescent that drug use will not be tolerated. Seek the help of Alcoholics Anonymous or another organization that deals with addictions. Ask your family doctor to identify community resources to help with this problem. Your health insurance may cover treatment for drug problems. Do not ignore drug use of any kind. It is a family problem and must be addressed.

(286) How should I discuss sexual issues with my adolescent?

More adolescents are becoming sexually active at younger ages. Therefore, sex education is needed at an early age. Check out what sex education topics are covered at your adolescent's school. Review these materials to know what he is learning. Discuss the topics with him in a one-on-one setting in which he can express his concerns and questions. Discuss the biological and emotional sides of sexuality. Because your adolescent will get information from his friends and acquaintances, provide more accurate information. Give him books to read that will enhance your discussions.

A typical adolescents feels he is invincible and nothing will happen to him. As a result, he takes risks. Emphasize the real physical consequences of sexual behavior: pregnancy, sexually transmitted diseases, AIDS. Talk about the emotional consequences of sexual behavior. An adolescent often will engage in sexual behavior as a way to gain acceptance or prove himself. Opening lines of communication with your adolescent will help you strengthen his self-confidence. You want him to feel free to discuss these issues with you when they arise. Share ideas on how to handle certain situations. This may help him resist the temptation to engage in sexual behavior before he is ready.

(287) How can my role model affect my adolescent?

Your model is an important variable. If your adolescent knows that his mother has spent the night with a man or that his father is living with another woman, he will tell you there is nothing wrong with sex outside of marriage. If he has witnessed his parents involved in multiple relationships, then he will think that practice is acceptable. Your model of sexual abstinence is important.

If you suspect your adolescent is sexually active, discuss the consequences of this behavior. You will have to decide about offering assistance to ensure safe sex. You may be torn between your value system that would emphasize abstinence and the reality of your adolescent's choices. It is hard to accept your adolescent's sexuality. Seek the counsel of a minister or family therapist.

(288) What resources are available to help me deal with critical issues I face with my adolescent?

Schools can provide many helpful resources for dealing with your adolescent. Teachers and counselors can discuss issues with you and recommend books, videos, or support groups. Your family doctor may be able to refer you to specialists or agencies that can help you deal with critical issues. Your minister and church programs may be excellent sources of support. Contact your local United Way or other community agencies for information on support in your community. The phone book may include help lines for different issues. The volunteers on the help lines can provide support or refer you to other sources of help. New technology has also contributed sources of support. Consult web pages and chat rooms for support.

Emphasize the importance of family.

Your adolescent may downplay the importance of her family in an effort to appear independent. She appreciates your interest in her life, as long as you don't try to intervene. Scheduling family meal times and organizing family outings will get more difficult as your adolescent develops more independence. Finding time for visitation with the absent parent will be more difficult as well. Special problems may develop related to the gender of the parent and your adolescent. Providing support to compensate for lack of contact with an absent parent can alleviate this problem.

(289) How can I get my adolescent to spend more time with the family?

Try to establish a certain day of the week for a family meal. Plan a monthly outing and block it off on your calendar. You may occassionally allow exceptions for attendance, but you need to show the importance of family by sharing time together. Include your adolescent's friends in some family meals or outings. Schedule a family outing to share a special event such as a younger sibling's Little League game or an older sibling's chorus performance. Take advantage of evenings when no one has plans. Have a celebration with popcorn or a night out for pizza.

(290) How can I help my adolescent balance her need for visitation with the absent parent with the need for time with her peers?

Visitation schedules may have to be adjusted for your adolescent. Encourage her to address the issue directly with the absent parent instead of trying to use you as a go-between. She may be afraid of hurting the absent parent's feelings, but she may also resent giving up her friends and activities to go for a visit. Model ways to discuss the issue. Offer suggestions for balancing time spent with friends and parents.

Suggest less frequent visitation but more phone contact between visits. Your adolescent should learn to take responsibility to initiate the phone contacts. She can set up a "phone visit" each week to catch up on activities. If your family has internet access, she can share news and jokes via e-mail. Another solution is to include friends in visitation whenever possible, either for a shared activity or an overnight visit. It may be possible to rotate visits. This way, the absent parent can have individual time with each child. Your adolescent can schedule which weekend she will have available to visit with the absent parent.

(291) How will my adolescent adjust to a single-parent home?

Your adolescent will likely rebel against parental restrictions. You as the custodial parent will bear most of the responsibility for enforcing these restrictions, which can put quite a strain on the parent-child relationship and can create great stress on the whole family unit. Encourage the absent parent to work with you for a solution that will be beneficial for all family members.

If your adolescent threatens to move in with the noncustodial parent, it can be emotionally devastating to you. However, chances are, if you tell him it is alright, he will probably change his mind. If he does follow through with his threat, changing living arrangements may provide an opportunity for you to spend more time with other family members to repair the damage from constant conflict. In some cases, it may benefit your adolescent to spend more time with the absent parent.

(292) What kinds of special issues will my adolescent daughter experience?

If you are a single mother with custody of an adolescent daughter, your daughter may be more at risk for developing problems in relationships with men. She may feel abandoned or rejected by her father. Missing out on being "Daddy's little girl" can lead to difficulties in establishing interpersonal relationships. Your daughter may seek male attention in unacceptable ways. She may be needy and will try too hard to please boys and men. She may be unable to trust men, causing her to be bitter and have difficulty establishing relationships with males. She may be attracted to older men in search of a father figure. For her emotional development, your daughter needs opportunities to maintain a relationship with an absent father. If this is not possible, then she needs substitutes such as a grandfather, uncle, or other male family member.

Your role model in relationships with men is very important for your adolescent daughter. You need to model a friendly relationship with her father. The interactions you model with him and other men in your life are important to show your daughter how to have successful relationships. Be careful when including your male friends (dates) in your family life. Your daughter may want to please them and will compete with you for their attention. She may also suffer from rejection when these friends are no longer part of your life.

If you are a single father with custody of an adolescent daughter, your daughter may have problems expressing some personal feelings. It is hard for an adolescent girl to discuss her budding sexual maturity and feelings with her father. She may have difficulty fitting in with her same-gender peers unless she has had a female role model to help her develop gender-appropriate interests such as clothes.

Your role model in relationships with women, including the absent mother, will affect the way your daughter relates to boys and men in her life. A close relationship with you could interfere with her ability to relate to boys her own age since they appear immature. Don't be too overprotective; this can scare off suitors.

(293) What kinds of special issues will my adolescent son experience?

If you are a single mother with custody of an adolescent son, he may develop an identity crisis due to his father's absence from his everyday life. He needs a father to show him how to be a man. He will try to imitate his father. He will learn how to relate to women by observing interactions between his mother and father.

Your son may have difficulty learning commitment if his father has fled commitment. Project completion, goal attainment, and stable relationships may suffer. Your son needs opportunities to maintain a relationship with the absent father. If his father is not available, then other male family members or male leaders in scouts, sports, or church activities may serve as role models.

If you are a single father with custody of an adolescent son, he may have difficulty developing a healthy relationship with the opposite sex. An adolescent boy is driven by his hormones and peers to "score." You need to model appropriate respect for and interaction with women. Provide an opportunity for you and your son to discuss these issues. Open lines of communication can help your parenting problems.

If your son has not had the opportunity to be around females, he may feel uncomfortable. He needs female contact to practice social skills such as manners and conversation. Learning to dance may improve his social standing. Significant female others can provide information on how females perceive issues.

(294) How can I help my adolescent develop healthy relationships with members of the opposite sex?

Model appropriate behaviors with members of the opposite sex. Your adolescent will learn from your example. Demonstrate a caring friendship for the other parent. Your adolescent should learn that there are all kinds of relationships between members of the opposite sex, that not all relationships have to be sexual. Spend time with other families and couples who can model healthy relationships. Your church group may be an excellent source of activities for families.

Instill good values.

The most important gift you can give your adolescent is a set of values to guide his choices in life. You cannot teach values. Schools cannot teach values. Values are learned by example. When you live your values, your adolescent will learn to live them as well. Discuss your values with him. Tell him how they affect your choices. Expose him to good role models.

(295) Who are adolescent role models? What effect can they have on my adolescent?

Your adolescent may have a variety of role models. They may come from everyday contacts (ex.: teachers and coaches) or from the media (ex.: sports figures and music stars). Your adolescent may try to imitate her role models. If she chooses role models who value education, she will put forth greater effort in school. If she chooses role models who smoke or use offensive language, she may copy these behaviors.

Be aware of who your adolescent chooses for role models. Look for clues such as posters or magazine articles in her room. Listen to what she says. She will frequently quote things her role models say. Encourage interest in positive role models. Provide opportunities to share time with them or learn more about them. Try to ignore negative role models. The more you object, the more desirable the individuals will become. Youth have very fickle loyalties. Try to expose your adolescent to other role models that may distract her.

(296) How can I protect my adolescent from making mistakes?

You can't protect your adolescent from making mistakes. And you should not protect him from the consequences of his mistakes. You can provide information and model good choices, but in the final moment of truth, it is up to your adolescent to make his own choices. You can limit his exposure to some dangers, but as he expands his horizons, you can't control all of the variables.

You want to protect him from making the same mistakes you did at his age, but this is not possible. Avoid lectures or confrontation. Help him evaluate the consequences of possible choices, and then let him make his own decisions. Avoid power struggles. Allow freedom as he proves himself trustworthy.

If your sense of trust is violated, enforce your values. If your adolescent comes home drunk, use reasonable and logical consequences—and stick with them. Take away privileges for a period of time if needed. Your consistency, model, and support are all valuable in helping him learn to make good choices.

(297) How can the experience of my own adolescence help my adolescent?

Remember how you felt when you were an adolescent. You probably would not want to live those years again, but they provided valuable lessons in how to become an adult. You now have the questionable privilege of living it again through your own adolescent. Provide guidance based on personal experience. You don't have to share everything, but do let your adolescent know that we all make mistakes. Just as you survived adolescence, your offspring will survive it and emerge as a mature adult.

Conclusion

Adolescence is a roller-coaster ride between childhood and adulthood. As your adolescent struggles to define himself, you rush to adjust to an ever-changing set of demands. You need resources for support in meeting these challenges. Understanding adolescent development will help you understand the difference between behaviors under parental control, such as use of a car, and those under hormonal control, such as mood swings.

Surviving adolescence means choosing your battles carefully. Allow your adolescent to control his choices. Intervene only in areas essential for his safety, such as using alcohol, and in future decisions, such as his education. Learn how to keep communication lines open regarding your adolescent's social life without interfering. If you forbid contact with certain friends, your adolescent will be strangely drawn to them. Model the importance of family. Help him understand and participate in family budget decisions. Allowances and part-time jobs can help him develop money management skills.

Work with his middle school as it provides extra motivation for your adolescent and also training in problem solving and life skills. Assist the efforts of his high school as it guides your adolescent in decision making for the future and developing independence.

Visitation

The 8th grader got off the school bus at her mother's house today. Her father left on a business trip this morning. He had included a new set of markers in her backpack from his home office to use for her school social science project. She had completed the outline for her report when she stayed with her mother last weekend. Last night at her father's house he had helped her "surf the net" to find information. She forgot to pack her printed notes in her backpack at her father's house this morning, but she could walk down the street to his house before dinner and pick them up since he lived only two blocks away. The notes could help her start a rough draft of her report at her mother's house tonight.

Not all single-parent families can provide this much support. Time and distance factors can intervene. A good relationship with the absent parent, however, can be an important contribution to growing up successfully in a single-parent home. Each parent will have different parenting styles, but children will benefit in different ways from their relationships with each parent. Children need to understand and accept different family structures. They need to see their families as safe and loving places for all family members. They can belong to and be loyal to more than one family at a time.

Allow for separate families.

Learning to be a family member is a challenge for anyone. Learning to be a member of separate families can create confusion for your child. She needs to learn, at her own level, about the issues of custody and visitation. She should realize that because one parent has more responsibility for her day-to-day activities, it doesn't mean the other parent doesn't care. She needs to understand that there are limitations on visitation because of schedules or distance, not because she is unloved or unwanted.

(298) How should I explain visitation to my child?

If possible, decide who will live where before any changes are made in parental living arrangements. In the presence of both parents and your child, calmly explain the pending changes. Emotionally charged issues surrounding changes often make this an impossibility, but your child will feel less stress if these issues are discussed as soon as possible. If it is not possible for both parents to participate in the discussion, then explain the changes yourself.

(299) How should I answer questions from my child concerning the absent parent?

Some of your child's questions will be easier to answer than others. He will want to know where the absent parent has gone and when that parent can visit. Set up a visit as soon as possible so your child can see where the absent parent is. Provide some special toys for your child to leave at the absent parent's house. This will help develop a sense of security because he will know he will be able to return. Emphasize that he has one home and family to be with most of the time and another home and family to visit.

(300) How can I prepare my child for visitation from the absent parent?

Treat visitation as a normal event. Put it on your family calendar. Help your child pack a bag of necessities for the trip away. Buy extras of some items, such as a toothbrush and a night light, that can be left at the absent parent's home. Put matched outfits with all accessories and underwear in separate plastic bags to cut down on confusion and also provide a place for dirty laundry.

Don't build expectations about the visitation. You can end up with an overexcited child who is difficult for the absent parent to manage, or you can end up with a very disappointed child if the visitation is canceled.

(301) How can I help my child adjust after visitation with the absent parent?

When your child returns from visitation with the absent parent, don't ask a lot of questions. "Did you have a good time?" or "I'm glad to have you back" is enough. Your child may worry about showing loyalty and be uncomfortable sharing information.

The absent parent may try to make up for the limited amount of time he/she spends with your child by lavishing him with special activities. Your child may return exhausted and "wired." Provide an opportunity for him to calm down and return to your family routine. Let him tell you or a friend all about his visit. Provide some "down time" before you request assistance with unpacking his bag or other routine chores. Offer your welcome home with hugs and kisses, but don't be hurt if your child seems distant for awhile. This is probably a form of "jet lag" caused by the transition from one environment to another.

(302) What should I do if my child wants to spend more time with the absent parent?

Explain to your child that visitation at the other home isn't the only time available to spend with the absent parent, and that the absent parent can be as involved as he/she chooses to be. Encourage your child to invite the absent parent to all performances, school events, and functions. Provide other ways for her to keep in touch such as phone calls or letters. Access to computer e-mail can allow frequent contacts.

(303) How can I deal with conflicts with the absent parent?

Sometimes the absent parent may use your child as a pawn in a chess game. This can be a power struggle over unresolved past issues or new issues—which is an unfortunate state of affairs. It can become the perfect example of a lose-lose situation. Your child loses because he feels caught in the middle between his parents. Loyalty issues can create too much stress for him. Both parents lose as a result.

Refuse to play the game. Communicate privately with the absent parent on issues before or after visits. Use written communication. Have a third party around to prevent the likelihood of confrontations. Ask a friend to greet the absent parent and pick up your child, or arrange for the absent parent to pick up and return your child to a neutral site such as a day-care center or restaurant so as to avoid unpleasant confrontations.

Ignore hurtful comments made in your presence. Contact the absent parent after a visit if your child reports discomfort over things the absent parent said. Try to negotiate an agreement to handle your differences without involving your child. Seek mediation or counseling if needed. Family courts have programs to help you deal with these issues in a way that protects your child.

(304) What should I do if I think my child has been neglected by the absent parent during visitation?

Susy was going to see Daddy. She was so excited. It was near Christmastime, and she was waiting for Santa Claus. She had not seen Daddy in several months, and she hoped to get some Christmas presents. She had left smiling and excited.

The little girl was returned after the weekend visitation with her father in the same red party dress she had worn to see him two days earlier. She looked tired and frazzled. Her hair had not been brushed in two days. She still had on the white stockings with the red patent leather shoes. She was brought into the hotel lobby with no coat on. When her mother hugged her, it was clear that she had slept in the dress for the past two nights. It was damp from her wetting the bed at night. Her shoes were damp, too, and the lines across her feet indicated she had slept in them.

Immediately address issues of neglect, danger, or abuse. Contact someone with the local family court to discuss your concerns and rights. Parental rights are protected legally, so you may not be able to refuse visitation without legal support. Neglect can be harder to prove than other forms of abuse, but if your child does not want to go with the absent parent, the issue must be for safety purposes. For example, if an absent parent has been drinking and arrives to pick up your child, calmly suggest another visitation date, or stall and ask for police intervention. These situations can be very traumatic for your child, but when issues of safety are involved, you have no choice.

Accept the absent parent's lack of involvement.

Moving out of the house and leaving a child is difficult for any parent. The absent parent may overcompensate and spoil your child to make up for the absence or else withdraw and avoid contact.

If the absent parent moves a great distance away, regular visitation may fall by the wayside. When the parent does visit, stress may result in unpleasant and angry exchanges between the two of you. Saying goodbye after each visit may be too painful to continue visitation, or the absent parent may become distracted by a new life and slowly drift away. The addition of a significant other may contribute to the problems. Conflicts with a stepfamily can force your child's parent to make a choice.

Even if the absent parent is not involved in your child's life, the parent still loves your child; other things have gotten in the way of their relationship. No matter what the source of the problem, the relationship between your child and the absent parent will suffer.

(305) How can I help my child handle disappointment if the absent parent misses visitation?

Mary's father dressed her in a pretty blue dress and put a new bow in her hair. She was all ready for her visit with her mother. It was always painful to say goodbye, so he left her and her backpack on the couch by the living room window while he went in the other room to read the newspaper. He fell asleep over the paper and didn't notice that Mary's mother was late. Mary was watching expectantly out the window. She would jump up and down with excitement every time she heard a car go by, and then slump down in disappointment as it passed her house. When her father awoke an hour later, he walked into the living room and found a tearful Mary. How could her mother do this to Mary again?

Keep your child busy. Have his bags positioned by the door early, and then distract him with a favorite TV show or game. When it is obvious there will be no visitation, allow him to express his feelings. Listen, but do not make negative comments about the other parent: "I know you feel disappointed that your mother could not make it today. I am sure she is disappointed about it, too." If your child is older, encourage him to draw a picture or write a note to the absent parent. This will show him that he can initiate contact. Provide an activity to take his mind off the missed visit: "Since you will be having dinner here, let's make a pizza together."

(306) What should I do if the absent parent repeatedly misses visitation with my child?

Rick was sitting at the window. It was Saturday, and he would get to see his father. He lived with his grandmother, and she had told him that his father was coming. He had awakened early because he was too excited to sleep. He was nervous because sometimes his father didn't come, but he just knew that if he wished it, it would happen this time. At lunchtime his grandmother came in and asked him to eat some lunch. He had not moved from the couch in fear that if he took his eyes off the driveway, his father would leave if Rick did not run out (as he had done once before).

Rick was not hungry, so he stayed on the sofa, looking out the window. Hours passed. It was now around 4 o'clock. He couldn't give up. Rick knew his father would come, if he just wished it some more. Around 5 o'clock, tears streamed down his face. His father didn't come. He ran out of the house so his grandmother could not see his tears and his shame of being unlovable. He went down the road to his friend's house. The boys there made fun of him because his father did not come. He felt aggressive and got into a fight with the boys. Their father made him feel worse by blaming him for the fight. The other boy's father called Rick a troublemaker. That night he couldn't sleep; he cried silently in his room.

Your child can have serious problems with self-esteem if visitation is missed all the time. If missed visitation becomes a pattern, avoid telling your child when visitation is scheduled. Let visitation, when it does happen, be a pleasant surprise. Also seek professional or legal advice.

(307) How can I encourage the absent parent to be more involved in my child's life?

When the absent parent calls or comes to visit your child, let your child's needs come first. Don't use the opportunity to bring up old issues or nag about new ones such as late child support payments. Focus on your child's transition from time spent with you to time spent with the absent parent. Use this opportunity to share important events that will help stimulate a discussion between the absent parent and your child, such as: "Mike lost another tooth this week"; or "Jane made a goal in her soccer game last night."

(308) How can I maintain the absent parent's presence in my child's life if that person is not available?

Your child will feel rejected and abandoned when the absent parent is not available to spend time with him. You can lessen these feelings by teaching your child ways to include the absent parent in his life without requiring the parent's presence. Have your child draw pictures or write notes to put in a box of things to save for the absent parent. This box of mementos will provide a bridge between your child and the parent. The memento box will be especially meaningful if the absent parent does make a visit; your child can take it along to show off the treasures. Provide addressed postcards or large envelopes, and encourage your child to write to the absent parent. If possible, mail the cards to the absent parent to help encourage a bond. If it is not possible to mail them, then place them in the memento box. Assemble a scrapbook in which you include pictures of family activities with the absent parent and also any letters or gifts from the absent parent.

(309) What should I say if my child expresses hatred for the absent parent?

Your child knows that the absent parent may be treated as a scapegoat for no other reason than his/her absence. If your child expresses hatred for the absent parent, especially one who doesn't maintain contact, listen quietly. Use passive listening strategies such as eye contact to let her know you are listening. Use reflective listening strategies to show you care, for example: "You seem to be saying that you are angry at your father for not visiting"; or "You seem to be saying that your mother made you feel uncomfortable by insulting your father." Do not probe or ask questions.

Give your child a chance to express her feelings. When her anger subsides, reassure her of the absent parent's love with statements such as: "Parents can love their children even when they do not spend time with them"; or "Parents may forget a visitation date, but they still love their children." Help your child clarify her feelings by saying: "You may be angry at your father, but you can still love him"; or "You may be disappointed in your mother, but I don't think you hate her." Avoid lectures or moralizing that discount your child's feelings, for instance, "It's not nice to hate." The goal is to support your child through a difficult emotional time.

Maintain family connections.

Visitation means more to your child than blocks of time spent here and there. It is a lifestyle of living in a larger family. If your child is able to maintain contact with the absent parent's family, he will feel more secure. He will feel a sense of belonging to the family, even though visitation with the absent parent may not occur. The larger family can make up for some of the security an absent parent may not provide.

(310) What kind of relationship should my child have with the absent parent's family?

It is important to include the absent parent's family in your child's life. Aunts, uncles, cousins, and grandparents can provide an important link to her family traditions. Their presence in your child's life can add to her feelings of safety and security. Their presence is particularly important if the absent parent is not available for visitation or parenting responsibilities. Extended family members can provide role models and tell stories about the absent parent as a child.

If the absent parent's family members live too far away to be included in your child's life on a daily basis, they can keep in touch by phone or mail. Have your child send them pictures and letters. Make suggestions about ways to maintain contact with the absent parent's family members. Remind family members that their time and attention are more valuable than money and toys. Encourage grandparents to write family stories or make a copy of the "family tree" for your child. She needs to feel connected to both sides of her family.

In some cases the absent parent's family may feel the need to choose sides and may not feel comfortable maintaining contact. If the absent parent's family members do not choose to be part of your child's life, include them in a scrapbook so that she can understand her family history.

(311) When the absent parent has chosen not to be involved in the life of my child, how do I encourage that parent's family to be involved?

"Why don't I see my grandpa—you know, Dad's father?" asked Johnny. His big brown eyes were filled with concern. Grandparents Day at his school was fresh on his mind. His mother's father lived a long distance away, but his father's father lived nearby.

His mother knew these questions would come one day and she was never going to be ready, so she took a deep breath and did the best she could: "He follows your father in choosing not to see you. I'm sorry, Honey. Some people live their whole lives and never really figure out what's important." She added with humor and a tickle, "I know what's important, and it is YOU!"

Johnny asked her the same question several other times in the next few days. Her answer was a variation of the same information each time. She knew that he didn't need more information but was still trying to process the answer she had given him. After several days of asking this question and several answers with the same variation, Johnny announced his understanding of the family problem: "When I have children, I am never going to leave them. I am going to be there for them when they have school plays and when they play soccer."

Your child's grandparents will have to make their own decisions concerning involvement in his life, regardless of the involvement or lack of involvement of their son or daughter with their grandchild. They still have the obligation to be grandparents, and each decision is an individual decision. In the instance of your child, no group or family decisions can be made. Just as each person answers for his/her own deeds, each member of the family must make personal choices and will remain responsible individually for those choices. Encourage each member of the extended family to be involved with your child, but realize you are not responsible for their choices.

Inform your child's school.

School officials need to be informed about custodial and visitation issues concerning your child. Teachers and counselors can provide support for her. They need to be aware of special circumstances such as a scheduled father-daughter tea at school that might upset her.

(312) Why should I inform my child's school of visitation arrangements?

Informing the school of visitation schedules is important. Teachers often note behavioral changes just before and after scheduled visitation times. One child seemed to have a problem settling down on Monday morning after a weekend with his mother, the absent parent. The teacher was able to set aside time for him or send him to a counselor to talk about his experiences until he was ready to handle schoolwork. If teachers are not informed, they may interpret the behavior as disruptive and punish your child. Teachers may be alert to changes in social, emotional, or academic behavior and in turn will inform you of these changes.

(313) Does my child's school need proof of custody?

Present official documentation of custody for the school files. School officials are required to release your child to either parent unless they have this documentation. This means if the absent parent arrives at school to pick up your child, the school does not have to notify you. Typically, schools will send copies of all records and permission forms to the custodial parent. It is the responsibility of the custodial parent to give copies of this information to the absent parent. Schools will meet with either parent to discuss student progress and problems and will accept signed permission forms from either parent unless court documentation is on file.

(314) Should I inform my child's school about personal family issues?

Because your child probably spends more "awake" time with her teachers than with you, teachers are in an excellent position to observe her behavior and provide support during times of stress. Meet with them to discuss issues that might affect her. Teachers can plan activities that are sensitive to her situation or make modifications to include all children. One teacher invited her husband and brother to visit the classroom and substitute as the father for children who had no father to invite to a father-daughter tea. Informed teachers may also include stories about single-parent families in reading class or arrange for your child to attend special support groups for children in single-parent families.

Conclusion

Your child can learn to belong to more than one family at a time. Encourage her to develop a relationship with the absent parent through visitation and phone or mail contact. Work with the absent parent to avoid unpleasant visitation experiences and provide a smooth transition and consistency. If the absent parent cannot be depended on to fulfill promises of visitation, help your child feel loved by gaining support elsewhere. Count on extended family connections to help fulfill these needs. Contact school personnel. Teachers and counselors can address special issues as they arise.

Abandonment

The 2nd-grade boy had packed his action figures and some food and clothes in his backpack and then started out the door. His mother stood at the kitchen door collecting her wits as he sobbed hysterically. The past couple of hours had been difficult. She couldn't even remember what had sent him off into hysteria. "I'm going to live with Dad; he loves me more than you do!" he screamed at his mother.

The mother recognized that this anger was a result of Johnny's feelings of abandonment. His father had not seen Johnny in more than a year. Johnny loved his father, and this abandonment was hard on him, particularly since he had seen his father riding around in a new car from time to time. Boys at school who spent time with their fathers on Saturdays made fun of boys who didn't. Johnny was going in search of his father so he could talk about his Saturdays with Dad.

Since Johnny's mother knew about abandonment feelings and their effects on children, she recognized that Johnny's threat of leaving was not an attack on her. It was her child's desperate struggle to feel worthwhile. She told Johnny in a quiet and supportive way: "Children in our family don't run away. They have never run away. It is not our tradition, and it is not accepted in this family. However, I do understand some of what you feel. Yet I cannot really know how you feel because I am not you."

She gave him some time to calm himself, and then she continued: "I think we should do something fun today that you choose, and then tonight you can write your father a letter and tell him how you feel."

When a parent leaves the home and is no longer physically present, children will feel abandoned. Regardless of visitation arrangements, they feel the loss of the daily presence of that parent. Their safe and secure world is shattered. Their physical and psychological development can be damaged.

When children do not feel safe and secure, they may exhibit short-term symptoms such as illness or behavior problems. These behaviors are often attempts to gain the attention of both parents. Since children cannot put their feelings into words, they will act out their anxiety. Both parents need to work together to find out what is causing behavioral changes and to give reassurance of their love. Children need to know that their family, even though it has changed, is still a safe and secure place.

Watch for symptoms of abandonment.

The little boy awoke screaming. He was babbling in terror as his mother reached his room. He grabbed her hair and buried his face in it. He must have been crying for a while because he was soaked. He had had the same nightmare every night for more than a month. "My daddy's all burned up! Help him! Help him!" he screamed.

The nightmares had begun several months earlier, shortly after Johnny's father left. Johnny's mother had informed the father, both at his office and through his attorney, that Johnny was having serious stress over the separation and needed to see him. However, the father remained unavailable.

One day Johnny's mother watched the video "Bambi" with Johnny. Through Johnny's comments, she detected a parallel between the forest scene with Bambi and the little boy's night terrors. She seized the opportunity to tell him that it was only a story.

Since Johnny was only 4, it was difficult to explain the difference between fact and fantasy. She explained to him that Bambi's father didn't die, that he just went away—like Johnny's father. He didn't die, he wasn't burned, he wasn't hurt, he wasn't sick—he just went away. The only part Johnny seemed to understand was that Bambi's father was okay. He had identified with Bambi through the thinking of a preschooler to help make sense of his father's disappearance. The insight of his mother helped her screen his movies and stories more carefully, and to be more available to explain the things he did see.

Your child has a hard time talking about feelings because he doesn't have the words to express his feelings. His behaviors are signals of his feelings. Different feelings can result in the same behaviors, and it is sometimes difficult to tell which feelings cause which behaviors. In addition, your child does not think the way you think. His sense of logic and cause and effect is very different. He may feel responsible for the loss of a parent.

(315) What does it mean for my child to feel abandoned?

If your child feels abandoned, he feels as though he doesn't count. He doesn't feel valued in his family or world and may feel unloved. He may exhibit this feeling by sulking or withdrawing. Since your child is very egocentric, he may feel guilty and responsible for the absence of one parent. Feelings of guilt may lead to withdrawn behavior.

Acting-out behavior can also come from feelings of abandonment. If your child's needs for emotional security are not met, he may become angry. This anger can lead to physical and verbal aggression. Acting-out behavior can lead to punishment, which adds to the feelings of being unloved. Teach your child to talk about his feelings and communicate his anger in a positive way.

(316) Why does my child feel guilty when she is not responsible for a parent leaving?

If your child wishes for something to happen and it does, then she thinks that her wishes made it happen. She may truly believe that she accidentally wished a parent away (after a scolding or a consequence administered by that parent). Guilt feelings can be compounded if she heard her name used during disagreements or arguments between her parents.

Your child probably thinks the world and its events revolve around her, just as early scientists believed the sun revolved around the earth. But just as astronomers became more knowledgeable and were able to prove that the earth rotates around the sun, as your child matures, she will be better able to distinguish events she creates from ones she does not.

Your job is to fill in the blanks and explain the reasons why there is only one parent in the home. Don't focus on your child's behaviors. Explain the changes in family structure in terms of adult choices and needs, for instance: "Mommy and Daddy both love you, but we needed to make a choice about what would make us feel better. This is the choice we made. We both want you to be happy and will always love you."

(317) Why is my child so sensitive to rejection?

"Bears are like boys," said Johnny confidently. He had just heard the story of Fuzzy Bear. Fuzzy Bear missed his Daddy Bear. Daddy Bear had gone to a new home in another forest. Daddy Bear had a new family. He still loved Fuzzy Bear, but he did not visit him. Daddy Bear was busy with new BabyBears and the LittleBears that lived in the new home. The other forest was also quite a distance away. In his heart, Fuzzy Bear would always love Daddy Bear. Fuzzy Bear was also certain that his Daddy Bear would always love him, too, even if he didn't visit.

When a parent leaves the home or your child first realizes his family is not like other families, he may suffer a trauma that is equal in emotional impact to the death of a parent. Regardless of the level of visitation by and contact with the absent parent, your child will feel the loss of the parent's day-to-day presence in the home. His feelings of safety and security are shattered. He will be sensitive to perceived rejection by others. If you are dealing with your own emotions and are less available to your child, he will feel rejected by you. If friends or relatives decrease contact during this period of change, he may feel rejected by them as well. Your child's behavior during this period can alienate other children and lead to even more feelings of rejection.

(318) How can I teach my child to handle rejection?

To your child, the loss of a parent is the ultimate betrayal. This can be a real event, such as the parent who never visits, or a perceived event, such as the parent who has a new family but continues visitation. In both cases, the abandonment is real to your child.

It is important for you to model ways to handle these feelings of rejection. Show your child that it is sometimes okay to cry. Tell her how much you love her and how much the absent parent loves her. Talk about your feelings; encourage your child to talk about hers. Be careful, however, not to use her as a confidant or therapist. Your role is to model verbal communication of feelings so that you can understand her view of the situation. This will allow you to clear up any misunderstandings.

Take care of the whole family.

The little girl stomped around the kitchen. As usual, she was demanding attention. Her older brother sat quietly on the sofa playing with action figures. He was in a world of his own. He was always so quiet. This time something clicked, and the mother noticed his withdrawn behavior. She realized that he had become a loner since his father moved away and that if she didn't change things now, one day she would have a teenager who spent his time away from the family. Perhaps as an adult he would go his own way.

"It is Johnny's turn," the mother said to Suzy. "It's not your turn anymore. I will help you again later." The mother did not intend to be cruel, but she wanted to change Suzy's behavior. The look of surprise on Suzy's face told the mother that she should have been more fair with her time. Johnny stopped playing alone and looked up, trying to evaluate the situation. "Johnny, come with me, please. We are going to spend some time together. Help me bake a cake."

Over the next few months, it was difficult to get Johnny out of the habit of spending time alone, but his mother was resolved to change the pattern. Every day she called for Johnny to come out of his room. "I'm playing," he would reply. "Well, you have played for 15 minutes, and I need your company. Come to the kitchen. Bring your toys with you."

Months went by with little gain. The mother was always coaxing Johnny to be with the family. "Small steps," the mother would repeat to herself, "I only want to make small steady steps."

A year later, Johnny now seeks out his mother. She has time for him and listens to his anecdotes about the boys and girls at school. He tells her everything. He shows her his collection of action figures and shares his schoolwork problems with her. He is more evenly competitive with his younger sister who used to steal the show. He now has a better relationship with Suzy and is not as jealous of her, but is more helpful with her. The family as a whole has prospered from Johnny's increased feeling of belonging and his elevated self-esteem. His more active contribution has created a happier family. The mother is now more careful to give equal time to everyone and also to give time to herself.

It is very easy to focus on your own needs or the needs of individual family members who are acting out. Sometimes you can lose sight of the fact that a family is more than just a collection of people. The family is a unit that depends on all its members to work together. The strength of the family is its ability to stand up in times of stress. Learning to focus on strengthening the family unit will help your family survive.

(319) How can I help my child overcome feelings of insecurity when I, too, am feeling insecure?

This is a difficult time for you. Raising your child alone is an overwhelming task. You may be suffering from feelings of abandonment and fear of the future. Trying to hide your feelings from your child probably will not work. At some point, the dam will break (usually during a crisis at home), and she will see you fall apart. This can be very scary for her. Help prepare her for this possibility by calmly talking with her from time to time about your feelings and needs.

(320) What should I do if I fall apart in front of my child?

If you lose control of your emotions in front of your child, call a friend or family member to come and help. This provides a calm adult to reassure your child during the crisis. If no one is available to fill this role, tell your child to give you some time alone. It will be a scary time for him, but you need time to deal with your emotions before you deal with him. Sometimes a family hug and crying together will help you.

When you are calm, sit down with your child and thank him for his love and understanding. Don't go into detail, but share your feelings. For example, say: "I sometimes feel as though I can't get everything done. That makes me so stressed out that I feel like I can explode. I know it scares you when I cry, and I'm sorry. But even adults need to cry sometimes. I feel better now, and I appreciate your understanding. Your love was the best thing to help me feel better." Show your love with a hug. Do a favorite family activity to show that everything is back to normal.

(321) What should I do if my child takes on an adult role?

If you are weakened emotionally, your child may take on extra responsibility to "take care of" you. The pressures of being the "man of the house" or your "friend," however, are not good for him. Reassure your child that you appreciate his offers. Discuss ways a family can work together to make it easier for all the members, such as sharing chores. Place emphasis on the family working together as a team. When your child becomes part of a team, he doesn't have to feel he is shouldering adult responsibilities.

(322) How can I let my child know he is safe?

Your child will feel safe and secure when he knows what is going to happen to him, for instance, what time he will have lunch, what bed he will sleep in, what the routines are on certain days. Provide consistency. Maintain family traditions. For example, continue "pizza night," choir night, or other traditions to maintain continuity in family life. Increase the presence of extended family and friends. Give your child opportunities to spend time with aunts, uncles, cousins, and grandparents from both sides of the family.

(323) How should I handle my own feelings of unhappiness and insecurity?

Do little things to make yourself laugh. Make your child laugh. Focus on the present day. In extremely sad times, focus on making it through the hour—set a timer to help you hang in there. Take it a minute at a time if you have to. Do not use friends and family members as sounding boards. This may damage future relationships with them. If they feel uncomfortable listening to you, they may withdraw and contribute to your child's feelings of rejection. If friends and family ask questions about the situation, do not discuss these issues in front of your child. If you need professional support, turn to a counselor, minister, or single-parent support group. Work out feelings in an environment with others who understand you.

(324) How can I avoid the empty-house feeling?

The single father worked at home on the computer in the afternoons so his children wouldn't need to go to afterschool day care. They usually allowed him to work undisturbed, but today they ran in excitedly. It was the last week in August, and school had just started. They wanted help to get into the attic. They felt it was time to decorate for Halloween. "It is not even Labor Day yet," he said. "When is Labor Day? Do we need to decorate for it?" they asked. He laughed; they were always so festive.

He reached into the cabinet above the refrigerator and brought down 50 American flags. They were small ones and had been used year after year. "Remember these?" "Yeah!" shouted the children. They ran outside with the flags to line the driveway with the little flags. Labor Day was a week away, but the decorations made the house and the father feel festive.

When a parent leaves, a house will "feel" his/her absence. The absence of the parent's contributions becomes glaringly obvious. In time, routines will change to adjust to this absence. The transition time can be easier if you fill those gaps. Bring a sense of festivity into your home. Celebrations don't have to be expensive. Invest in holiday decorations, and use them repeatedly. Turn on the radio and sing or dance together. Add a special homemade treat to your family meal. Make some popcorn and enjoy a movie or sports event on TV together. Take a hike at a local park. The main emphasis should be on enjoying family time. This will add to your child's feelings of security.

Establish a sense of trust.

It is important that your child reestablish a sense of trust after a traumatic event in her life. It takes time to develop trust. Be patient with yourself and your child. The betrayal of trust has a lasting effect, but you can learn to trust again, although not in quite the same way. Redeveloping trust is dependent on meeting emotional needs. Your child will feel the need to test you constantly, which can be stressful for you, but your patience will pay off in a more trusting relationship.

(325) How can I develop a sense of trust in my child when she feels abandoned?

Gina and Alli always got a chill when their mother left them. It was like a cold hand gripping their hearts. They each knew that the other felt the same way, for they had discussed it. Their father had left them. He never saw them again, though he was seen from time to time driving here or there. They knew their mother would not do the same, but something made them afraid. Their mother could sense this, so she always left her pager number for them. She spent all of her extra time with them so they would feel safe, but they never really completely trusted her not to leave forever.

Trust is built one step at a time. The first step to building trust is opening up lines of communication. When your child feels abandoned, she may withdraw from communication. Go to a special private place (your room, the backyard swing, or a place in the park) with her. Reassure her of your love for her and also that of the absent parent. Tell her that you know it is scary to change the family. Allow your child to share her feelings. Validate her feelings. For example, say: "It's okay to feel scared about being alone." Don't ask a lot of questions. Let your child know she is grown-up enough to discuss feelings. Schedule an appointment for another discussion. Suggest others who would understand her feelings, such as the absent parent, school counselors, and grandparents.

(326) What should I do if have to break my word to my child?

Keeping your word is the most important step toward building your child's trust. Don't mention things to others that you discussed with him in private. Follow up by keeping your appointments for additional shared time. Never make a promise you can't keep. A promise that "I will never leave you" is unrealistic. Your child may consider your business trip or evening out with friends as leaving him.

If an emergency arises, and you must reschedule an event with him, ask him to consider your options. Explain the facts, for instance: "My computer erased my file that was due on Thursday. If we go to the zoo, I will spend 6 hours with you. If we do not go to the zoo until Friday, I can spend these 6 hours recreating my file. I will have the work done again, and I will get a raise. A raise means that we will have extra money every month to help us pay bills and have some extra fun. Then we can splurge on an extra treat at the zoo! However, if we go to the zoo on Thursday and I don't get the work done, I probably will not get a raise. What do you think is best for our family?" Get your child to participate in the rescheduling. Then keep your word of honor!

(327) What should I do if my child doesn't talk about her feelings?

If your child does not open up and talk about her feelings, offer her books for single-parent children that can open the door to discussion. Read age-appropriate books about families together. Discussion of characters in books is an excellent way to encourage your child to relate her own feelings.

(328) How can the use of fictional characters help my child deal with the feeling of abandonment?

"Will I get to hear about Fuzzy Bear?" asked Johnny. "'I'm sure you will. Ask to hear about him, and I'm certain you will," Johnny's mother replied as they walked along the path to the family therapist's office.

The therapist was waiting near the door. "Hello," he called from the door. "I was just thinking about Fuzzy Bear! He has gotten into some difficulty, and I thought I might share it with you. Come in! Come in!" The grandfatherly gentleman waved goodbye to Johnny's mother. He and Johnny settled in for a nice story.

The family therapist told Johnny's mother that he would explain abandonment from Johnny's father through the stories of a little bear. The stories coincided directly with Johnny's difficulties. When Johnny was in trouble at school for fighting, so was Fuzzy Bear!

"You see," said the therapist, "Johnny can get the information he needs to solve his problems without the pain of being 'me.' It is the bear whose father has left, not 'my father.' But the information is there all the same. In time, when Johnny is ready, he will realize that the real character in the story is him. This way, Johnny understands his feelings in his own time frame, not ours."

Your child can relate to characters in a book such as Fuzzy Bear or Furrdinand the Furrballer. If Furrdinand the Furry has trouble with his friends making fun of him because his Furrdad is gone, your child will get the information without the pain of it being "me." When he is ready to accept his loss, he may realize that Furrdinand the Furry's problem is just like his. Puppets can also help your child open up and communicate his feelings. He probably will talk to puppets about things he can't express to adults. Let the puppet start the conversation.

(329) What is the most crucial part of maintaining the trust of my child?

Keep the lines of communication open. It is important that your child trust you when you promise to be available to talk. If you are having a bad day, tell her that you really do care but this is not a good time for you, and suggest a better time. This provides a model for your child and keeps her from feeling rejected. For example, say: "We all have bad days. Things were rough for me at work today, and I'm just too tired to think. I love you, and I know you have some things you need to talk about. Can we wait until after I have a rest to talk?" Keep your appointment and show your appreciation for her understanding. Let her know that family members support each other and you appreciate her support when you were tired.

Make your child feel loved.

The young girl was waiting for her daddy to return from work. She had let herself into the house and was doing her homework. She arrived at 3:30, and he would arrive at 6:00. She wished her mother had stayed with them, but she was living in New York now. She was a writer for a magazine, but she never wrote to Pamela.

Even though Pamela's father was devoted to her, Pamela felt as though her mother left because she was unlovable. Pamela mistakenly reasoned that if she had been lovable, her mother would not have left. This made Pamela feel as though she didn't fit in anywhere. These feelings affected her personality and were compounded when the other girls at school made fun of her.

A sense of belonging is fueled by unconditional love. Unconditional love provides the reassurance that "no matter how bad things get, there still will be someone who loves me." Your child will test you to make sure you love him. He may ask for constant reassurance. Remember, a family is the place where you are always loved, no matter where you are or what you do. First, meet your child's physical needs. Then give him a sense of security and belonging

(330) What can I do to make my child feel loved?

One of the best ways to make your child feel secure is to make her feel loved. Physical touch (a pat on the head, hugging, or kissing) contributes to feelings of being loved. Tell your child, "I love you" every morning and before bedtime each night. If you cannot be with her, leave a note or picture to remind her of your love. Also take opportunities during the day, such as waiting in the grocery line, to remind her. Give your child a hug or compliment. Tell her how special she is. Write notes on napkins to place in her lunchbox or notebook. A smile can convey a lot of love and acceptance. Remember, love is unconditional—"just the way you are."

(331) What should I tell my child if he asks if the absent parent loves him?

Let your child know that the absent parent loves him, although the absent parent may not show it in a way your child can understand. Offer a simple explanation and redirect his attention to your love for him. For instance, say: "Yes, your father loves you. He is just confused right now. He doesn't know how to show you that love. He is the one missing out, because you are the best thing in my life. I get to enjoy my time with you. I am lucky. He just doesn't know what he is missing right now." It can be very difficult to keep your response neutral or upbeat when you are feeling your child's pain. Keep it simple. Negative comments about the absent parent can affect your child's self-concept.

(332) What should I tell my child if she asks if I will ever stop loving her?

If your child asks if you'll stop loving her, she is probably afraid you will leave her. After all, she reasons, if her parents don't love each other anymore and have separated, then they may stop loving her and leave her. It is hard to explain different kinds of love to a child. Some of the following explanations may help:

- "Sometimes people can love one another and not like to do the same things. This makes them want to separate."
- "Sometimes people are in love, but they change what they like to do, and then they aren't happy together. They go separate ways and find other people they enjoy spending time with."
- "Sometimes people decide they would be happier if they didn't live together. This can be a very hard decision when you have children, because both parents love their children and do not want to leave them."

Explain to your child that her parents' love for her is different than their love for another adult, that her parents can see themselves in her and their love for her continues to grow each day even though they may not like some of her behavior. Assure her that even when you are not with her, you carry love for her in your heart.

Allow expression of feelings.

Your child acts out his feelings. If he is feeling bad, he may exhibit a change in behavior. He may become quiet and timid or make excessive demands for attention. He will have different responses depending on his age and temperament, so give support to deal with his feelings or stress accordingly.

(333) How can I help my child if he becomes withdrawn?

Johnny was acting as though he wanted to be alone. Every time his father would ask him to participate in something, he would say, "Leave me alone," or " I don't want to." His father was mistaken in thinking that Johnny needed time to be alone to get over his mother moving out. With time, things got worse. Finally, Johnny's father talked with the school counselor.

The counselor told Johnny's father, "Activity interrupts depression." The phrase stuck in his mind. After that, he continually coaxed Johnny into a game of cards, or a game of ball, or a visit to the ice cream parlor. If Johnny couldn't be coaxed, his father would sit with him while he played or watched TV and interrupt him constantly, saying things such as, "Can you believe that?" or "What do you think of this?"

His father knew that it had taken months for Johnny to become withdrawn. Johnny was angry that his mother had remarried and now was busy with a new stepson. His father accurately reasoned, "It will take at least as many months of support to bring him back out, one step at a time." By summer vacation, with a lot of support, Johnny was saying, "Come on Dad, let's play ball!" Johnny's father was glad to oblige.

If your child becomes excessively quiet and withdrawn, intervene. He needs your attention. Initiate parent-child or family activities such as board games, storytime, or a ballgame. Introduce a pet into the family. Research shows that children who own pets have more outgoing personalities and make friends more easily. Pets also provide unconditional love and attention. Taking a pet for a walk provides opportunities for social interaction with neighbors and friends. Talk about a new puppy or kitten can bring excited children to your home to break up withdrawn behavior. If a dog is not suited to your lifestyle, a hamster or rabbit may work.

(334) How can I avoid the tendency to react only in times of obvious need of my child?

When there is too much on the agenda, the things that squeak (or scream) are taken care of first. It is an act of survival. This is the reason you may allow a withdrawn child to spend time alone. It is easy to ignore a withdrawn child who is not actively seeking your attention in the chaos of everyday life. If there are no demands from her, you may think, "If it isn't broke, don't fix it." Conversely, the longer you wait to provide attention to a withdrawn child, the more withdrawn she may become, and the longer intervention will take to change the behavior.

Management strategies will help you become a more efficient parent. The panic of having too much on your agenda will dissipate as you change your parenting style. You can then take advantage of periods of free time to initiate shared activities with a withdrawn child. Take turns with her choosing activities. Remember, she needs your attention, even if she doesn't demand it.

(335) What should I do when my child makes excessive demands for attention?

Cindy missed her mother's attention. She had put together puzzles, jumped rope, played with the dog and rabbit, and ridden her bike, but her mother was still working on the computer in the home office. Cindy had been in school all day and missed her mother. She was angry. She was also hungry. She went into the office and demanded to eat. "I'm hungry, and I'm not afraid to tell you!"

Her mother, who was working on an important deadline, evaluated the demand. The clock showed that it was past dinnertime. Feeling the demand was appropriate, the mother responded sweetly, "Did you say you were hungry?" Cindy was immediately sorry for her tone of voice and said, "Mommy, I'm so hungry, I have a stomach ache."

> *"Then let's eat! In fact, it will save time if we order a pizza. Is cheese okay?" Cindy waited for the pizza delivery while her mother continued to work. Cindy brushed away tears of stress. She had been afraid to demand her mother's attention. She knew that this deadline would provide an account that was important to the family's finances.*

When your child demands excess attention, it can be very irritating. He always seem to be underfoot. He may whine, have temper tantrums, or break things. It is tempting to address the negative behaviors and yell at him. This only makes negative behaviors stronger. A demanding child will welcome any attention, even if it is punitive. Anything is better than being ignored. It may be difficult with demanding behaviors to remain calm, but it is most effective. If your child's behaviors are not dangerous or destructive, then ignore them. Behaviors may get worse at first, but your child will finally give up if he does not get rewarded with your negative attention.

Sometimes interruptions are warranted. At times, you can simultaneously continue your work and give in to your child's demands to a certain degree. For example, go to the public library, sit near the children's book section, and work on your laptop computer or make business calls. This is a win-win situation—your child is entertained and enriched, it is free of cost, you are able to work, and you are in the company of librarians who will help remind your child of his manners.

When interruptions are not warranted, a simple verbal reminder of a more appropriate behavior choice may work, for instance, "Interruptions when your mother is on the phone are rude. A child who quietly waits for his turn will have a chance to talk to his mother when she gets off the phone." Nonverbal cues such as the "Shh" sign may help redirect the behavior.

(336) What should I do if my child becomes destructive to get attention?

If your child engages in dangerous or destructive behavior, immediately remove her from the situation. For example, if she is throwing food across the dinner table, stop the behavior. Firmly move her to an area where she can sit and think about her choices. A few minutes alone can prepare her to rejoin the family. If she is still upset, allow a few more minutes for reflection.

(337) What is the best strategy for managing my child's excessive attention-seeking behavior?

Amanda walked up to her mother, knowing she was on a company deadline for work. Amanda hated it when her mother worked at home. She wanted to go to the Donut King and buy donuts, some with pink icing and sprinkles for herself and some with chocolate frosting for her brother. "I want to go to Donut King!" she demanded. Her mother looked up and said, "I have a deadline; I can't go today, but we can go tomorrow." "I want to go now!" Amanda demanded. Her mother apologized for her lack of time and went back to work.

Amanda left her mother alone for the next two hours. She did her homework and worked on her reading log. She then made a set of flash cards with her week's spelling words. Her mother noted with admiration her independent and constructive behavior and made a quick phone call.

There was a knock at the door. "Yoo Hoo," said Sally. "Where's the princess?" Sally was Amanda's favorite neighbor. She lived next door. "Can I take Amanda for a ride?" asked Sally. "She would love to go to Donut King," confided Amanda's mother. "Well, let's go!" said Sally. Off they went. Amanda was rewarded for working independently and constructively, not when she was demanding.

Amanda came back with donuts for her mom and brother. She was praised and admired for her good manners.

Give your child attention when he is behaving appropriately, not when he is misbehaving. It is easy to overlook him when he is playing quietly. The quiet play provides a pleasant break for you. This is the best time, however, to stop what you are doing and tell your child how much you love him. Provide specific praise for good behavior, such as: "You two have been playing very well together. It is more fun for everyone when you are taking turns and sharing." This rewards quiet behavior.

(338) Should I show love for my child when he is exhibiting unacceptable behaviors?

The preadolescent boy ran up to his mother in the parking lot of the local putt-putt golf course. Out of breath and with a worried look on his face, he said, "There were these big boys, and they were making fun of us, and they threw their golf clubs at us, and we weren't having fun, so we quit playing golf and got a rain check."

The mother replied in a manner to defuse this obvious game: "If that really happened, then we will never come back here because the clientele is not suitable for children. However, if it is just a little tall tale to have fun, then I guess we can come back."

The look of surprise on the boy's face was interesting. He had a choice: he could admit it was manipulation on his part, or he could give up going to his favorite place. He quickly said, "Okay, it was just for fun. Let's go trade in the tickets I won for prizes!"

The mother normally gave her son attention when he had a problem, so he came up with lots of problems. Since he was really bright, he could think of many ways to keep her unnecessarily involved in his life. What had started out as overprotectiveness to keep him from further hurt after his father left had turned into a game on his part to keep his mother involved in his life at a very intense level. Joseph was now underachieving in school, and his mother had been looking for answers. After reading several parenting books, she was able to recognize her role as the enabler and as a result changed some of her parenting strategies.

In this situation Joseph's mother had been careful to give him a way out that preserved his dignity rather than lowering his self-esteem by calling him a liar. In response, he had easily accepted her redirection, since his ego was not at stake. She wondered how many times she had responded to his need unnecessarily by overreacting. She began to feel that she would get a handle on preadolescence after all!

You are the adult. You have to keep your cool. Tell your child that his behavior is unacceptable, but you still love him, for instance: "I love you, but lying is not acceptable. You need to tell the truth so I can trust you." Label the behavior, not the child: "You are a good boy, but lying is bad. You need to choose to tell the truth."

(339) What should I do if I lose my cool over unacceptable behaviors exhibited by my child?

It is natural to lose your cool sometimes when your child exhibits unacceptable behaviors. This is the time to take a cool-down period to gain control. For example, say: "I love you, but I am having a hard time dealing with this behavior. I am going to my room to cool down. I will discuss this with you when I am calm."

(340) What should I do if I feel angry and have a short fuse?

"Parental time-out" is an important intervention strategy. It can prevent a cycle of physical or verbal child abuse. If you are angry, you are more likely to use physical punishment or say things that are emotionally destructive. Verbal attacks can damage your child's self-esteem. Remember, you are the adult, and you need to be in control of your emotions first. If you cannot calm down, call a friend or a help-line to give you support and redirect your parenting efforts.

(341) Why does my child get angry when I'm sick or I don't feel well?

Your child may be frightened by your vulnerability and will act out his feelings of insecurity because he doesn't know how to deal with a sad, tired, or sick parent. He may act out of control, running around or picking fights with siblings. This can create a crisis in the home. Call a babysitter, friend, or relative to take over your family responsibilities for a while. Your child's needs for attention can be met, and you can take a break.

(342) Why does my child try to take advantage of me when I seem vulnerable?

If your child is younger, she may not understand how much some comments can hurt, for example, "A good mother would . . ."; or "If you loved me, you would . . ." If she is approaching adolescence, she may push buttons to get a response. For example, the comment "I don't want to grow up to be fat like you" is intended to elicit emotional rather than intellectual responses from you. You may feel guilt or anger. As a response to these attacks, you are more likely to say something you don't mean.

Don't get hooked into a fight. Tell your child when her words hurt you. For example, say: "It makes me angry when I hear that I am not a good mother. I think I can be a good mother even if I don't drive you to the mall right now"; or "It makes me feel sad when I hear that I don't love you because I won't let you have a pet"; or " It hurts my feelings when someone calls me fat." Nondefensive responses put your child in a position to apologize for her hurtful words. Remind her that apologies don't always take away the hurt, that she needs to stop and think before she makes such comments.

Conclusion

Understanding your child's feelings of abandonment will help you understand his behaviors. He may withdraw or act out in response to his feelings of rejection. He will generalize his feelings of aban-donment by one parent to fear the loss of your presence. He needs reassurance that he can trust you to be there. Help him reestablish this sense of trust. Give him love and emotional support.

Even though you should allow a child who is feeling abandoned to express his feelings, don't permit him to dominate the family. Take care of the whole family, including yourself and your feelings of insecurity and abandonment.

Parenting for the Future

The mother was rushing hurriedly around the house finishing laundry and checking off lists. Her youngest daughter was due to leave for college the next morning, and there were so many things to do. It seemed there were heated verbal exchanges every few minutes. The mother was anxious and kept lecturing her daughter on what to do and how to do it. Her daughter was bristling with resentment. She was an adult now and didn't need her mother acting like she used to do before summer camps. The evening passed quickly.

In the hustle of the morning when the father came to pick up his daughter for the trip to campus, there was no time for a real goodbye. The single mother looked around the empty house. She bent over to pick up an orphan sock and held it to her eyes as she began to cry. She had heard about the empty-nest syndrome, but she had been so busy with all the tasks to be accomplished, she hadn't taken time to think about the true meaning of this event. Her children were adults now. Her youngest was taking off from the nest. They didn't need her anymore. Her nest was empty, and her heart was heavy.

Time passes quickly. It seems that one minute you are hustling from one child's soccer game to another child's music lesson, and the next thing you know, you come home from work to an empty house. There is no one to chauffeur, feed, clean up after, scold, or hug.

It happened gradually in some ways. They began to spend more time with friends. Then there were part-time jobs after school and dates. First one child left the nest and headed for college or a job, and then the next child. You rejoice as your children bring home their special friends to meet you, and you cry as you watch them go down the aisle to be married.

Suddenly you find that you have free time. For single parents, this is a new experience. Some parents make the mistake of trying to hold on to their children too long. They call to check in and constantly offer help with laundry, finances, meals, and so on. Pretty soon, instead of an empty nest, they find themselves in a rubber nest. Their children keep bouncing back between jobs or spouses. Grandchildren become a part of the household. Parenting adult children with children of their own creates a whole new set of challenges.

Other empyt-nest parents quickly fill their calendars with activities to keep themselves occupied. They put more effort into their careers and develop hobbies and relationships. They maintain contact with their children but offer a listening ear rather than nosy intrusion.

Prepare your child
for vocational success and
economic independence.

Success on the job is a developmental task of adulthood. Economic factors may intervene to keep your child from accomplishing this task, however. You may feel guilt over failure to help her develop appropriate vocational goals and complete educational programs to prepare her for economic independence.

(343) How can I help my child understand the work ethic?

Understanding the work ethic begins at home. Teach your child responsibility for personal care and possessions and responsibilities within the family. You may link pay to performance and adjust weekly allowances according to timely and quality completion of chores. Remind your child that the family must complete all chores before fun activities begin. Model your work ethic, as in the following: "Father has to mow the lawn before we can go to the ballgame"; or "Mother has to finish a project at work because her boss is depending on her." Reinforce pride in your efforts, such as: "I feel proud of the cake I made for your birthday. It really looks and tastes great"; or "You must really feel good about the way your room looks. You did a good job of cleaning it up today."

(344) Should I be involved in my child's future job choices?

When a child is young, he has unrealistic career aspirations. As he matures, he will try out many different career aspirations. Provide guidance and support in your child's vocational planning. Help him address career goals before entering high school. Educational choices made during the high school years have long-standing consequences. Your child will be eager to take classes and graduate with his friends. Over-ambitious choices may cause stress and even failure, which can lead to threats of dropping out of school. Taking easier educational tracks, however, can limit the choices available upon graduation.

(345) How can I help my child make appropriate vocational choices?

Support the efforts of your child. Listen to his ideas about careers that interest him and why. Provide assistance in researching these careers. Enlist the help of school counselors and public librarians to help guide your child toward appropriate resources. Locate mentors who will allow him to "shadow" them on the job for a day and interview them about their careers. Investigate a mentorship program.

(346) Will a mentor help my child?

A mentor will spend time weekly with your child to provide support and motivation. Such a relationship can be very beneficial for her. A mentor provides an adult role model other than teachers to reinforce parental messages about education and values.

(347) Will volunteer work help my child make career choices?

Volunteer work related to your child's career choice can provide long-term rewards in experience and decision making for the future. Work experiences at a hospital or with veterinarians, builders, mechanics, or other professionals may be available for him to explore different vocations. School clubs, organizations, and church groups provide many volunteer opportunities.

(348) How can I help my child prepare for economic independence?

Preparation for economic self-sufficiency begins when your child is a preschooler. Teach her to take care of her own needs, such as dressing and feeding herself, and to participate as a family member, such as in helping with chores. Increase expectations of skills as she matures.

As your child reaches adolescence, conflicts over fulfilling these tasks will emerge. Previously mastered skills may be forgotten. Parental persistence in maintaining standards, while avoiding power struggles, is a difficult balancing act. The skills mastered in childhood and adolescence, however, will provide your adult child with a firm foundation in maintaining economic self-sufficiency.

(349) How important is it to teach my child money management?

Teaching your child to manage money is an important step toward his developing economic independence. Learning the value of money can be a difficult lesson, however. Money may seem to burn a hole in his pockets because he has a difficult time delaying gratification. He will learn to live on credit at a very early age, as evidenced in this statement: "Mommy, I promise to pick up my toys if you'll buy me an ice cream cone now!"

(350) How can I help my child practice money management?

Give your child opportunities to practice money management. Give her an allowance (tied to chores or not) or pay her for doing chores or extra jobs. Train your child to set aside some money for savings and charitable contributions. As with everything else, the way you model money management will have the most impact on her. Make her aware of financial choices such as comparison shopping and the cost of using credit. If she seems to believe in the "magic money card" that allows one to get cash or goods when needed, verbalize that the card is not "magic"—the bill must be paid each month; its power is linked to the strength of one's bank account.

(351) How can I teach the concept of banking to my child?

Open a savings account for your child. Try a joint checking account when he is old enough to take some responsibility for his expenses. Make sure the account includes a requirement for both signatures. The concept of balancing a checkbook may take a while for him to grasp. He may bounce checks because he forgot to write checks in the register or subtract after each check. Debit cards can compound the problem because he may pull out the card when he doesn't have the checkbook available and then forget to record withdrawals. He may use the debit card to check his balance—and then spend the balance. Teaching the concept of waiting for checks to clear is difficult to teach a teenager who lives in the present. This also presents a problem in handling credit. Your child needs to see the total amount paid for an item on credit—both the number of payments and the cost of the payments.

(352) What should I do if can't afford to help my adult child with finances?

It is difficult to watch an adult child struggle financially. You may be able to provide emotional support, but financial resources may not be available. Do not risk financial security for your retirement or put yourself in financial risk. Even if you have the resources, it may not be in your child's best interests for you to bail him out. He needs to learn from experience. You may help him locate resources or support systems to help him through difficult times. Free consumer credit counseling resources can provide expert advice on how to handle financial problems and may also provide services in intervening with creditors. Social work agencies may provide other sources of assistance. Helping your child manage independently is more helpful than making him feel dependent on you.

(353) Where should I draw the line between helping my adult child and being an enabler?

Provide unconditional love and support. Be willing to help out in times of trouble, but don't protect your child from the consequences of his behavior. He needs to deal with his own debts, or he will continue to live beyond his means. The same is true for other situations. Practice tough love. Love your child by letting him face the consequences of his behavior.

If your child continues to have difficulties in interpersonal relationships, don't sympathize. Rather, suggest looking inward for the cause of the problem. Some personal behaviors may be the cause of the problems. Remember, loving your child enough to let him grow up is the most loving thing you can do.

Foster commitment and intimacy.

Concern over your child's emotional problems can lead to guilt on your part. You may have an especially difficult time dealing with guilt over the possible effects of single parenting on her emotional development. She may carry the emotional scars of growing up with an absent parent into adulthood and develop problems with self-esteem and interpersonal relationships. Teach your child about commitment. Prepare her for emotional maturity.

(354) How can I help prepare my child for commitment?

Commitment is a part of intimacy. Your child will learn commitment from both role models and experience. Your model of commitment to your child and to other relationships is the first experience of commitment she will have. You model commitment when you maintain contact with your parents and siblings and when you continue your relationships with friends who have a hard time, such as going through a divorce. Teach by example that commitment means staying in a relationship even when the going gets tough.

Commitment is also a part of success in a life endeavor. The ability to stand up for what you believe in and to stick with a task until completion are both examples of commitment. Model commitment to charitable causes or to your job. Follow through on tasks around the house.

(355) How can I teach my child to stick with a task?

Require your child to share in responsibilities in the home. Assign tasks that are reasonable for her developmental level. Insist on her finishing each task. Check to make sure the task is completed to her best ability. For example, she may not rinse the dinner dishes as well as you, but she needs to be rewarded for putting forth the effort. Praise her for showing commitment to a task, for example: "You did a good job of remembering to put out the trash last night. You didn't need to be reminded"; or "Your room wins the clean room award today. You certainly did your best." Likewise, have your child face the consequences for not following through with a task. You may need to send her back (sometimes with your direct supervision) to complete a task correctly. You may need to enforce a consequence as in: "You forgot to feed the dog this morning, and he was hungry all day. You will care for your dog tonight instead of going to play with your friends."

(356) How can participation in extracurricular activities help my child learn about commitment?

Your child needs to understand that his team or organization depends on him. He must fulfill his commitment, even if it means missing a great TV show or someone's birthday party. If your child nags to participate in activities and then whines about having to go, you may want to consider having him pay for the activity. Make a deal that if he fulfills the commitment and you don't have to listen to him complain about going to practice or other required activities, you will pay him back at the end of the season.

(357) How can I help prepare my child for intimacy?

The ability to develop intimacy in a relationship is a developmental task of adulthood. It is a prerequisite to the ability to nurture one's own children. Provide your child with emotional security and love to help prepare him for intimate relationships in the future. Model communication and caring.

(358) How can I help my child develop emotional maturity?

Emotional maturity is difficult to define. It is a process rather than a point in time. Emotional maturity includes the ability to develop and maintain interpersonal relationships. It includes skills such as communication and commitment. Ownership of behaviors and facing the consequences of behaviors are important aspects of emotional maturity. An emotionally mature adult is responsible and nurturing. Your role model is the most powerful tool available for developing emotional maturity in your child. Provide reinforcement when she demonstrates mature behaviors such as giving up toys to a younger playmate or stopping to help a friend in need.

Adapt to changing roles and family situations.

You can provide an excellent role model and training in independence for your child in his early years, but you cannot control the choices he makes as an adult. Life choices such as careers, marriage, and divorce made by your adult child will affect the role you play as a parent. You need to learn to adapt to these roles.

(359) What should I do if my adult child is making poor life choices?

It is very difficult to watch your child make poor life choices in her career and personal life, but avoid lecturing or moralizing about such choices. Avoid the use of "I told you so." You cannot control the choices she makes. Do not feel responsible for them. Continue to give unconditional love, but don't try to protect her from learning from personal mistakes. Learn to accept the things you cannot change.

(360) What is my role as an in-law?

You look forward to that special moment when your child marries and forms his own family. A wedding marks a change in his role—he is now a husband. It also marks a change in your parenting role.

You become an in-law. There are many jokes about in-laws. They usually focus on in-laws who are too intrusive.

You may feel a void when your child focuses on his new family. You begin to feel excluded, especially as a single parent. Give your child space and time to develop the new relationship. Keep your advice to yourself. When holidays arrive, let him develop new traditions in the new family. Resist the temptation to use guilt to get him to share the holidays with you. If you are invited to join the new family (and possibly the other in-laws) for celebrations, avoid imposing your traditions.

You may still maintain contact and offer invitations, but expect some resistance at first. Your patience should pay off as your relationship with your adult child grows. The birth of a grandchild can provide an especially close bond.

(361) How can I cope with my adult child's divorce?

If your adult child divorces, it can be a particularly painful time for you. You may feel guilt because you were not able to model a lasting marital relationship. You may feel like a failure as a parent because your child did not develop the emotional maturity to maintain a marital relationship. Drop the guilt. You provided the best model you could. You provided the nurturing and support to help her develop emotional maturity. The responsibility for the final choices she makes belongs to her. Instead of worrying about who is to blame, help her through this difficult time. This is a time when she really needs your unconditional love and acceptance and a listening ear. Because you can understand some of the problems your adult child faces, especially if children are involved, you can be her strongest support.

(362) What is my role as a grandparent?

The same rules apply for you as a grandparent as apply for you as a parent of a married child. Offer support, but do not intrude. You may spoil your grandchild a bit, but don't undermine his parents' efforts to be independent and to do things their way. Try to keep your rules from differing too much from those of his parents. For example, avoid giving guns as gifts (no matter how much he begs) if the parents object. You may, however, stretch the rules a bit and let your grandchild have an extra cookie just because you love him. This is your chance to enjoy stages in child development that you were probably too busy to notice with your own child. It may be your chance to see the ultimate "revenge"—living long enough to see your grandchild do to his parents what his parents did to you!

(363) How can I be a good grandparent if my adult child divorces?

Regardless of your child's relationship with his child or the child's other parent, you still have the power to determine your role as a grandparent. Be as committed a grandparent as you are a parent. Single parenting is not for the weak-hearted; neither is grandparenting a single-parent child. Maintain your values. Your role as a grandparent is much more needed in the life of a single-parent child.

Accept your parenting role as a lifetime commitment.

Parenting for the future begins in infancy. Daily dedication as a parent provides your child with a firm foundation for the future. Individual choices you make along the way do not make or break the future of your child. There is no perfect parent. One parenting mistake (or many) will not scar your child for life.

(364) How can I help my child feel worthwhile?

Strong commitment, consistency, positive support, encouragement, a sense of values, and unconditional love are the parts of parenting that create a whole child who is confident and capable, sensitive and loving, independent and self-sufficient. Commitment to providing unconditional love is more important than individual daily events. Through commitment and love, many things can be worked out within your family.

(365) How can I handle all of my parenting responsibilities?

Do not take all of the credit—or all of the blame. Remember, parenting is a lifetime commitment. There are many variables such as temperament and other role models in your child's life that also influence his adult behavior. Remember, you are not alone. Turn to relatives, friends, support groups, and professionals for support and guidance. Look forward to that day when you and your adult child can become friends and share happy stories with your grandchild about the "good old days."

Conclusion

Parenting is a lifetime commitment. Your role is to do the best you can and seek outside help when necessary. Prepare your child for independence all along the way. Give training in specific skills such as money management. Provide support for vocational choices and related educational decisions. Foster commitment and intimacy to help prepare her for success in interpersonal relationships.

Learn how to relate to your child in a new way as she becomes an adult. Support her independence and ability to make decisions. Learn the difference between helping and meddling. Drop the guilt if she makes poor choices, but enjoy the rewards when she makes good choices.

Suggested Readings

Anderson, Hal W., and Gail Anderson. *Mom and Dad Are Divorced, But I'm Not: Parenting After Divorce*. Chicago: Nelson-Hall Publishers, 1981.

Anderson, Joan. *The Single Mother's Book*. Atlanta: Peachtree Publishers Ltd., 1990.

Appel, Karen W. *America's Changing Families: A Guide for Educators*. Bloomington IN: Phi Delta Kappa Foundation, 1985.

Bienfield, Florence. *My Mom and Dad Are Getting a Divorce*. St. Paul MN: EMC Corp., 1984.

Cohen, Miriam Galper. *Long-Distance Parenting: A Guide for Divorced Parents*. New York: Penguin Books, 1989.

Corneau, Guy. *Absent Fathers, Lost Sons: The Search for Masculine Identity*. Boston: Shambhala Publications, Inc., 1991.

Duvall, Evelyn M. *Family Development*. Philadelphia: Lippincott, 1971.

Erikson, Erik H. *Childhood and Society*. New York: W. W. Norton & Co., Inc., 1963.

Fassel, Diane. *Growing Up Divorced: A Road to Healing for Adult Children of Divorce*. New York: Simon & Schuster, 1991.

Fontana, Vincent J., and Valerie Moolman. *Save the Family, Save the Child: What We Can Do to Help Children at Risk*. New York: Penguin Books, 1991.

Hart, Archibald, D. *Children and Divorce: What to Expect—How to Help*. Dallas: Word Publishing, 1982.

Herman, Stephen P. *Parent vs. Parent: How You and Your Child Can Survive the Custody Battle*. New York: Pantheon Books, 1990.

Hill, Gerald A. *Divorced Father, Coping with Problems/Creating Solutions*. White Hall VA: Betterway Publications, 1989.

Hodges, William F. *Interventions for Children of Divorce: Custody, Access, and Psychotherapy*. New York: John Wiley & Sons, Inc., 1991.

Hansen, Ed. *Clinical Implications of the Family Life Cycle*. Rockville MD: Aspen Books, 1983.

Hass, Aaron. *The Gift of Fatherhood*. New York: Simon & Schuster, 1994.

Kline, Kris, and Stephen Pew. *For the Sake of Children: How to Share Your Children with Your Ex-Spouse in Spite of Your Anger*. Rocklin CA: Prima Publishing, 1992.

Leman, Kevin. *Bringing Up Kids Without Tearing Them Down*. Nashville: Thomas Nelson Publishers, 1995.

_____. *Making Children Mind Without Losing Yours*. New York: Dell Publishing, 1984.

Levine, Karen. *What to Do When Your Child Has Trouble at School*. New York: Reader's Digest Books, 1997.

Lieberman, Alicia. *The Emotional Life of the Toddler*. New York: Macmillan Publishing, 1993.

Mattes, Jane. *Single Mothers by Choice*. New York: Random House, Inc., 1994.

McCoy, Elin. *What to Do When Kids Are Mean to Your Child*. New York: Reader's Digest Books, 1997.

Miller, David R. *Single Moms, Single Dads: Help and Hope for the One-Parent Family*. Denver CO: Accent Books, 1990.

Nelson, Jane, Lynn Lott, and H. Stephen Glenn. *Positive Discipline A to Z*. Rocklin CA: Prima Publishing, 1993.

Pomerantz, Virginia. *The First Five Years: The Relaxed Approach to Child Care*. New York: St. Martin's Press, Inc., 1984.

Ricci, Isolina. *Mom's House, Dad's House: Making Shared Custody Work*. New York: Collier Books, 1987.

Rofes, Eric E. *The Kids Book of Divorce by, for, and about Kids*. New York: Vintage Books, 1982.

Shapiro, Robert B. *Separate Houses: A Handbook for Divorced Parents*. Lakewood CO: Book makers Guild, 1989.

Simmons, Monica. *Aster Jungle: Furrdinand the Furrballer*. Ft. Pierce FL: Longwind Publishing, 1998.

_____. *The Construction of Asterplanet*. Ft. Pierce FL: Longwind Publishing, 1998.

_____. *Aster Desert: CD Romina in the Silicon Valley*. Ft. Pierce FL: Longwind Publishing, 1998.

_____. *Aster Ocean: Dolfinia the Bottlenoze Dolf*. Ft. Pierce FL: Longwind Publishing, 1998.

_____. *Aster City: 2Kul 4Skul the Hyperspace Hero*. Ft. Pierce FL: Longwind Publishing, 1998.

Weinhaus, Evonne, and Karen Friedman. *Stop Struggling with Your Child*. New York: HarperCollins, 1991.

Weitzman, Elizabeth. *Let's Talk about Living with a Single Parent*. New York: Power Kids Press, 1996.

Bilbliography

Alessandri, Steven M. "Effects of Maternal Work Status in Single-Parent Families on Children's Perception of Self and Family and School Achievement." *Journal of Experimental Child* 54, no. 3 (1992): 417-33.

Astone, Nan Marie, and Sara S. McLanahan. "Family Structure, Parental Practices, and High School Completion." *American Sociological Review* 56, no. 3 (1991): 309-20.

Barrie, J. M. *Peter Pan*. New York: Viking Ariel Press, 1991.

Brewer, Barbara G., and Edna Rawlings. "Feminist Therapy with Single-Again Mothers: A Case Analysis. Special Issue: Psychotherapy with Women from a Feminist Perspective." *Journal of Training and Practice in Professional Psychology* 7, no. 1 (1993): 26-34.

Brown, Susan. *Parental Rights and Responsibilities*. Unpublished document, 1997.

_____. *Preparation and Implementation of Individual Education Programs*. Mt. Pleasant MI: Central Michigan University Dean's Grant, 1985.

_____. "Sciencing and Children with Special Education Needs." In *Sciencing*, ed. Sandra Cain and Jack Evans. Columbus OH: Merrill, 1984, 1990.

_____. "The Validity of SEARCH as a Screening Instrument for At-Risk Kindergarten Children." Dissertation, Georgia State University, 1979.

_____ and M. L. Anderegg. *EXC 304 Exceptional Children and Youth CoursePack*. Kennesaw GA: Kennesaw State University.

Caplan, Frank D. *The First Twelve Months of Life*. New York: Perigee Books, 1993.

Clarke-Stewart, K. Alison. "Single-Parent Families: How Bad for the Children?" *NEA Today* 7, no. 6 (1989): 60-64.

Compas, Bruce E., and Rebecca A. Williams. "Stress, Coping, and Adjustment in Mothers and Young Adolescents in Single- and Two-Parent Families." *American Journal of Community Psychology* 18, no. 1 (1990): 525-45.

Dawson, Patrice. "The Effect of the Single-Parent Family on Academic Achievement. A Review of Related Literature." *Review of Literature* (Illinois) (1981).

DeMaris, Alfred, and Geoffrey Grief. "The Relationship Between Family Structure and Parent-Child Relationship Problems in Single-Father Households." *Journal of Divorce and Remarriage* 18, no. 1-2 (1992): 55-77.

DiSibio, Robert A. "The Effect of the Single-Parent Family on the Academic, Emotional, and Social Achievement of the Elementary School Child." *Review of Literature* (New York) (1981).

Dreikus, Rudolf. *Fundamentals of Alderian Psychology*. Chicago: Alfred Adler Institute, 1960.

Edwards, Owen.*Working Woman Magazine*, September 1981, 53-57.

Entlewisle, Doris R., and Karl L. Alexander. "A Parent's Economic Shadow: Family Structure versus Family Resources as Influences in Early School Achievement." *Journal of Marriage and the Family* 57, no. 2 (1995): 399-409.

Fong, Margaret L., and Ellen S. Amatea. "Stress and Single Professional Women: An Exploration of Causal Factors. Special Issue: Women and Health." *Journal of Mental Health Counseling* 14, no. 1 (1992): 20-29.

Friedemann, Marie Luise, and Marian Andrews. "Family Support and Child Adjustment in Single-Parent Families." *Issues in Comprehensive Pediatric Nursing* 13, no. 4 (1990): 289-301.

Galinsky, Ellen, and Judy David. *The Preschool Years: Family Strategies That Work from Experts and Parents*. New York: Times Books, 1988.

Gelbrich, Judith A., and Evelyn K. Hare. "The Effects of Single Parenthood on School Achievement in a Gifted Population." *Gifted Child Quarterly* 33, no. 3 (1989): 115-17.

Glasser, William. *Schools Without Failure*. New York: Harper & Row, 1969.

Glenwick, David, and Joel Mowry. "When Parent Becomes Peer: Loss of Intergenerational Boundaries in Single-Parent Families." *Family Relations* 35 (1986): 57-62.

Goldberg, Wendy, A., Ellen Greenberger, Sharon Hamil, and Robin O'Neil. "Role Demands in the Lives of Employed Single Mothers with Preschoolers." *Journal of Family Issues* 13, no. 3 (1992): 312-33.

Goldstein, Robin. *More Everyday Parenting*. New York: Penguin Books, 1991.

Gottman, John. *The Heart of Parenting: Raising an Emotionally Intelligent Child*. New York: Simon & Schuster, 1997.

Grief, Geoffrey L. "Lone Fathers in the United States: An Overview and Practice Implications." *British Journal of Social Work* 22, no. 5 (1992): 565-74.

Gringlas, Marcy, and Marsha Weintraub. "The More Things Change . . . Single Parenting Revisited." *Journal of Family Issues* 16, no. 1 (1995): 29-52.

Hetherington, E. Mavis. "Presidential Address: Families, Lies, and Videotapes." Presidential address of the Society for Research in Adolescence. *Journal of Research on Adolescence* 1, no. 4 (1990): 323-48.

Hoffman, Lois. *Review of the Research*. Ann Arbor MI: University of Michigan Press, 1984.

Kaye, John, Diane Moyer, Denise Zecca, and Emil Soucer. "A Feminist Reaction to Fong and Amatea." *Journal of Mental Health Counseling* 15, no. 4 (1993): 461-64.

Konner, Melvin. *Childhood*. New York: Little, Brown and Company, Inc., 1991.

Krech, Kathryn H., and Charlotte Johnston. "The Relationship of Depressed Mood and Life Stress to Maternal Perceptions of Child Behavior." *Journal of Clinical Child Psychology* 21, no. 2 (1992): 119-22.

Koritt, K. A. "Family Therapy with One-Parent Families." *Contemporary Family Therapy: An International Journal* 13, no. 6 (1991): 625-40.

Kübler-Ross, Elisabeth. *Death, the Final Stage of Growth*. New York: Macmillan Publishing, 1969.

_____. *On Death and Dying*. New York: Macmillan Publishing, 1969.

Kurdek, Lawrence A. "Differences in Ratings of Children's Adjustment by Married Mothers Experiencing Low Marital Conflict, Married Mothers Experiencing High Marital Conflict, and Divorced Single Mothers: A Nationwide Study." *Journal of Applied Developmental Psychology* 12, no. 3 (1991): 289-305.

Lieberman, Alicia F. *The Emotional Life of the Toddler*. New York: The Free Press, 1993.

Lukken, Miriam W. *Read This Book Before Your Child Starts School*. Springfield IL: Charles C. Thomas, Publisher, 1994.

Marsh, Herbert W. "Two-Parent, Step-Parent, and Single-Parent Families: Changes in Achievement, Attitudes, and Behaviors During the Last Two Years of High School." *Research Report* (New South Wales, Australia) (1989).

Maslow, Abraham H. *Toward a Psychology of Being*. New York: Van Nostrand Reinhold, 1968.

_____. *Motivation and Personality*. New York: HarperCollins Publishers, 1987.

Mauldin, Teresa, and Carol B. Meeks. "Time Allocation of One- and Two-Parent Mothers." *Lifestyles* 11, no. 1 (1990): 53-69.

McCullough, Jane, and Cathleen U. Zick. "The Roles of Role Strain, Economic Resources, and Time Demands in Explaining Mother's Life Satisfaction." *Journal of Family and Economic Issues* 13, no. 1 (1992): 23-44.

McDermott, Kathleen R. "Single Parenting and Placement of Elementary Students: A Review of the Research." *Review Literature* (Illinois) (1990).

McKenry, Patrick, and Mark A. Pine. "Parenting Following Divorce: A Comparison of Black and White Single Mothers." *Journal of Comparative Family Studies* 24, no. 1 (1993): 99-111.

Measell, Richard, P. "The Impact of Coming from a Single-Parent Household on the Labor Force Plans of College Females: Some Economic and Counseling Implications." *Journal ofDivorce and Remarriage* 18, no. 1-2 (1992): 219-30.

Nelson, Jane, Cheryl Erwin, and Roslyn Duffy. *Positive Discipline for Preschoolers*. Rocklin CA: Prima Publishing, 1995.

Nelson, Jane. *Positive Discipline*. New York: Ballantine Books, 1987.

Olson, Myrna R., and Judith A. Haynes. "Successful Single Parents." *Families in Society* 74, no. 5 (1993): 259-67.

Piaget, Jean, and Barbara Inhelder. *Psychology of the Child*. New York: Basic Books, 1969.

Quindlen, Anna. *Raising Kids in a Changing World*. New York: Prentice Hall Press, 1991.

Rimm, Sylvia. *Why Bright Kids Get Poor Grades and What You Can Do about It*. New York: Crown Publishers, 1995.

Rissman, K. "Single Parenting: Interventions in the Transitional Stage." *Contemporary Family Therapy an International Journal* 14, no. 4 (1992): 323-33.

Ross, Julie A. *Practical Parenting for the 21st Century*. New York: Excalibur Publishing, 1993.

Roy, Crystal M., and Dale R. Fuqua. "Social Support Systems and Academic Performance of Single-Parent Students." *School Counselor* 30, no. 3 (1983): 183-92.

Rubenstein, Mark. *The Growing Years: A Guide to Your Child's Emotional Development from Birth to Adolescence*. New York: Athaneum Press, 1987.

Sanik, Margaret Mietus, and Teresa Mauldin. "Single- versus Two-Parent Families: A Comparison of Mother's Time." *Family Relations* 35, no. 19 (1986): 53-56.

Shelov, Steven P., and Robert E. Hannemann. *Caring for Your Baby and Young Child: Birth to Age 5.* New York: Bantam Books, 1991.

Stoppard, Miriam. *Complete Baby and Child Care.* New York: Dorling Kindersley Publishing, Inc., 1995.

Simon, Jane. "The Single Parent: Power and the Integrity of Parenting." *American Journal of Psychoanalysis* 50, no. 2 (1990): 187-98.

Snyder, James. "Discipline as a Mediator of the Impact of Maternal Stress and Mood on Child Conduct Problems." *Development and Psychopathology* 3, no. 3 (1991): 263-76.

Southworth, Nicki. "A Comparative Study of Single-Parent Children and Two-Parent Children in Behavior, Achievement, and Emotional Status." Master's thesis, Kean College, New Jersey, 1984.

Stolba, Andrea, and Paul R. Amato. "Extended Single-Parent Households and Children's Behavior." *Sociological Quarterly* 34, no. 3 (1993): 543-49.

Sundeen, Richard A. "Family Life Course Status and Volunteer Behavior: Implications for the Single Parent." *Sociological Perspectives* 33, no. 4 (1990): 483-500.

Thiriot, Toni L., and Eugene T. Buckner. "Multiple Predictors of Satisfying Post-Divorce Adjustment of Single Custodial Parents." *Journal of Divorce and Remarriage* 17, no. 1-2 (1991): 27-48.

Tillitski, Christopher, J. "Fathers and Child Custody: Issues, Trends, and Implications for Couseling. Special Issue: Mental Health Couseling for Men." *Journal of Mental Health Counseling* 14, no. 3 (1992): 351-61.

Turecki, Stanley. *The Emotional Problems of Normal Children.* New York: Bantam Books, 1994.

Vygotsky, Lev Semenovich. *The Collected Works of L. S. Vygotsky.* Trans. Rieber and Carton. New York: Plenum, 1987.

Watts, David S., and Karen M. "The Impact of Female-Headed Single-Parent Families on Academic Achievement." *Journal of Divorce and Remarriage* 17, no. 1-2 (1991): 97-114.

Westcott, Mary E., and Robert Uries. "Has Family Therapy Adapted to the Single-Parent Family?" *American Journal of Family Therapy* 18, no. 4 (1990): 363-572.